# The Una...

# HOW TO BEAT NINTENDO

# NINTENDO

## Gamebook

The Unauthorized

# HOW TO BEAT
# NINTENDO

Gamebook

## JON SUTHERLAND    NIGEL GROSS
## PAUL BOUGHTON

Boxtree

Many thanks to Newsfield Publications, publishers of The Games Machine, Crash, Zzap 64, Fear and Games Master International, especially Franco Frey, Oliver Frey and Jonathan Rignall.

Also Garry Williams, of ACE magazine, . . .

Thanks to Paul Shaw 'our' artist.

First published in the UK 1990
by BOXTREE LIMITED, 36 Tavistock Street,
London WC2E 7PB

1 3 5 7 9 10 8 6 4 2

© Jon Sutherland, Nigel Gross, Paul Boughton 1990

Typeset by Cambrian Typesetters, Frimley, Surrey
Printed and bound in Great Britain by
The St Ives Group PLC

**British Library Cataloguing in Publication Data**
Sutherland, Jon
1. Electronic games
I. Title   II. Gross, Nigel
794.8

ISBN 1–85283–075–1

# CONTENTS

## SHORT REVIEWS

# INTRODUCTION

Nintendo is a cult phenomenon. Around 35 million Nintendo Entertainment Systems have been sold worldwide in three years – 19 million in the United States. The Americans have dubbed it 'Nintendomania'.

And it's about to take Britain by storm.

If you already own a Nintendo Entertainment System you'll know what we are talking about. If you're thinking of buying one, what are you waiting for? The explosive, exciting, addictive world of Nintendo will blow your mind.

In either case you'll find this *How To Beat Nintendo* game guide essential reading. Games for this amazing machine are not cheap. Buying a bad game could prove a costly mistake. Likewise, buying a superb game and failing to conquer more than just the first couple of levels will also leave you feeling cheated.

That's where *How To Beat Nintendo* comes in. Not only is the most comprehensive critical guide to Nintendo games to be released in the UK, but it also contains a mass of hints, tips and advice on how to get the most from the games.

With exhaustive research and playtesting we believe How To Beat Nintendo is indispensable to all the gamers.

Let the good times scroll.

Jon Sutherland, Nigel Gross & Paul Boughton, 1990

# NINTENDO FACTS

● The Nintendo Company started as a playing card manufacturer 101 years ago.

● Tetris – a Nintendo program with sales of more than 100,000 copies on home computers in the United States – was designed in the Soviet Union by computer wizard Alexey L. Pazhitnov.

● Nintendo is the world's largest maker and marketer of video games. It controls 90 per cent of the home video market in Japan.

● Nintendo's 'Game Boy' system will be the next craze to hit the UK. This portable hand-held console features interchangeable game cartridges, and LCD screen, stereo earphones. Two Game Boys can be linked together for two-player action.

● By the end of 1989 it was reckoned one in five American households had a Nintendo Entertainment System. That's around 26 million NES consoles. Add to that a mind-boggling 101 million games sold.

● In America more than 80 game counsellors answer an average of 50,000 calls six days a week asking for game tips and strategies. A team of 20 also answer an average of 10,000 letters each week. A further 30,000 call Nintendo's custom service hotline.

● *Nintendo Power*, a bi-monthly subscription magazine, covering hints, tips and previews, has more than 1.2 million subscribers.

● Do you live, breathe and almost eat Nintendo? Well, they do in the USA. Hungry NES fans can buy two fruit-flavoured breakfast cereals, shaped like favourite Nintendo characters, and read game tips on the boxes. They're called Nintendo Cereal Systems.

● *The Super Mario Bros.' Super Show* is favourite weekday afternoon television viewing for NES fans. Not only does the show, which has live active with cartoons, feature the brothers Mario and Luigi, but also Link, the hero of the two Legend of Zelda games. A half hour series, *Captain N – The Game Master*, is also under development.

1

• There are more than 150 Nintendo games, not all are available in Britain – yet!

• Since 1987 more than 9.1 million copies of Super Mario Bros. have been sold in the US. Plus 3.5 million copies of Super Mario Bros. 2.

• Three million Legend of Zelda games have been sold in America since 1987.

• The first Nintendo Family Computer – the Famicon – was first sold in Japan in 1983. Two years later sales were more than 6.5 million.

• The NES was first introduced to America in 1985.

• Donkey Kong was a huge success in the early eighties. But why is it called Donkey Kong? Where's the donkey? Legend has it that the star of the game was based on the movie monster King Kong – check out the resemblance. Anyway, the game was called Monkey Kong but was mistranslated from the Japanese into Donkey Kong. A strange story . . . and possibly true.

• Nintendo proudly boasts a whole host of famous names among its millions of game players. They include Bros star Matt Goss, Paul McCartney, Cliff Richard, Ian Botham, Tom Cruise, Michael J. Fox, Tom Hanks, Bruce Willis, Goldie Hawn, Don Johnson, Robin Williams, Kurt Russell, Henry Winkler, Matthew Broderick, Whoopi Goldberg and Robin Givens.

## Jon's Nintendo Top 10

1. GAUNTLET
2. CONTRA
3. OPERATION WOLF
4. 1943
5. ZELDA
6. MIKE TYSON'S PUNCH OUT
7. SUPER MARIO BROS.
8. KNIGHT RIDER
9. PRISONER OF WAR
10. MICKEY'S MOUSECAPADE

## Nigel's Nintendo Top 10

1. SUPER MARIO BROS. II
2. LEE TREVINO'S FIGHTING GOLF
3. RC PRO-AM
4. CONTRA
5. DOUBLE DRAGON II
6. OPERATION WOLF
7. 1943
8. SPY V SPY
9. OTHELLO
10. IKARI WARRIORS

## Paul's Nintendo Top 10

1. SUPER MARIO BROS.
2. IKARI WARRIORS
3. OPERATION WOLF
4. CONTRA
5. BATMAN
6. DOUBLE DRAGON
7. DOUBLE DRAGON II
8. R-TYPE
9. ROBOCOP
10. SPACE HARRIER

# HOW TO USE THIS BOOK

When we started this book it was obvious that it would be necessary to divide the games up into some kind of logical order. What follows is an explanation of the categories that we chose. Inevitably some of you will disagree with the choices, but we hope the majority find them agreeable. Like most attempts at pigeon-holing there are a few games that simply defy the process. In order to accommodate these we have created a 'Non-descript' category.

SHOOT'EM UPS

As the name implies this category includes games based around the premise: 'If it moves shoot it!'. This is perhaps the largest single grouping of games on the Nintendo and may say a lot about the people who play them . . .

RACE'EM UPS

These are games where the player controls a car or other land vehicle. The action always involves travelling fast, and often shooting as well.

BEAT'EM UPS

Explore strange new worlds, meet exotic people – and beat the hell out of them. From karate to plain old punch-ups, if physical violence is your thing, then this is your category. Many contain elements of the Shoot'em Ups.

CUTESIES

Pretty-pretty graphics, minimal violence and plot lines with a lot of sugary sweet sentiment. Most of them are platform based adventures very similar in content to Arcade Adventures.

## ARCADE ADVENTURES

Games with elements of both Shoot'em Ups and Beat'em Ups, but offering a lot more in the way of puzzles and strategy. These games are almost always *big*, with hundreds of screens to explore.

## MAZE GAMES

Games that, one way or another, involve solving the puzzle of a maze!

## SIMULATIONS

The Nintendo endeavours to simulate reality! These usually fall into either the sports sim, or the techno sim. The first is self explanatory, the second involves driving cars, flying airplanes and so on.

## PLATFORM GAMES

These involve leaping around a series of platforms dodging nasty little things. They are closely related to Arcade Adventures, but are more limited in content. It is very common to come across Beat 'em Up/ Platform Game hybrids.

## INDESCRIBABLES

Games that defy pigeon-holing!

Well, that's listed the Icons used to show the types of game. We have also used Icons to describe the basic contents of the game:

## AGE SUITABILITY

The minimum age that we feel is suitable for a player. This, it must be stressed, has been judged purely on how hard the game is to play, not on whether the content is suitable for a particular age group.

## BRAIN POWER

Marks out of ten for how much thinking you will need to do during the game. The higher the score the more thinking involved.

## SLEIGHT OF HAND

Again a mark out of ten for how much manual dexterity is required for playing the game well. Scores of nine or more indicate a real joystick basher.

## CAUTION! BAD TASTE

Some games are, sadly, extremely violent. We have used this opportunity to draw attention to a few games that we feel go too far.

## LIGHT ZAPPER

Games that can be used in connection with the add-on Nintendo Light Zapper.

## NUMBER OF PLAYERS

Surprise, surprise . . . the number of players that can play the game!

When it comes to the game review itself we have again tried to be as systematic as possible, and as such every review follows the same format:

6

## REVIEW

A brief description of what the game is about.

## WEAPONS

Descriptions of the weapons at your disposable and hints on advantageous ways to use them. The term 'weapons' is used loosely!

## SPECIALS

Most games feature a number of special items that can help you win. These are listed here with what they do and occasionally where to find them.

## THE ENEMY

You will usually have some kind of computer-controlled adversary to beat, and this is where we tell you about him!

## HINTS

Useful hints and tips on how to play the game successfully.

## REMARKS

Our opinion on the game itself. We have not tried to be subjective, it's simply our opinion!

## COMMENTS

Any specific comments from the three authors.

## THAT'S NICE AND THAT'S A SHAME

Occasionally games had outstanding features that we either loved or loathed. Most don't have any of these but watch out for them when they do.

# A–Z Section of Games

6      8      7–70      1

## REVIEW

Practice makes perfect in this mix of maze, logic and zap. There are 5 rooms to explore in each level and 10 levels in all. And you start with 5 much-needed lives.

So say hello to Lolo, a prince on a quest to rescue Princess Lala from the Great Devil in his castle. Each level has a maze to explore, squares to be strategically moved and monsters to cheat and trap. Speedy thinking is vital. Special items in the game aid Lolo's progress. The aim of each level is to reach a chest and its jewel. If you succeed, all the monsters on that level disappear and access to the next level is gained.

## WEAPONS

**Heart Framers** offer protection to Lolo from the monsters and they can't be moved. If you capture all the Heart Framers the chest will open. **Special Heart Framers** contain a surprise. Capture one and you get two magic shots. **Emerald Framers** move around to block monsters. **Passes** are blocks with arrows on. Lolo can pass through these but not against the direction of the arrow.

## SPECIALS

**Magic shots** – hitting the monster will turn it into an egg, which can be safely moved for a brief period of time. **Power** (marked as 'PW') can be used to alter the direction of one-way passes.

## THE EMENY

*Gol* stays asleep until all the Heart Framers have been taken – then watch out! *Alma* – don't let it get too close. *Leeper* – bump don't jump. *Don Medusa* is slow with the sword. *Medusa* – if looks could kill. *Rocky* – well hard. *Snake* is surprisingly harmless. *Skull* is the same as Gol.

## HINTS

1 Trees will stop monsters, magic shot and Lolo.
2 Deserts will cut Lolo's speed.

11

**3** Bridges can be used by Lolo and monsters.

**4** Flower beds make a good hiding-place, but monsters *will* lurk.

**5** Lava is too hot to handle without a bridge.

**6** Try riding the eggs across rivers – but the current must be fast.

**7** Rocks will stop Magic Shots and monsters. For Lolo to pass through, the hammer must fall.

## REMARKS

Don't be put off by the 'young' look of The Adventures of Lolo. Grown-ups will be addicted.

## COMMENTS

PAUL: A seemingly simple game which is quite complex in the later stages.

THAT'S NICE: A chance to exercise the little grey cells.

THAT'S A SHAME: Younger gamesters might find this too complicated.

### AIR FORTRESS™

| 8 | 7 | 7–70 | 1 |

## REVIEW

Straight-forward, no non-sense, inter-galactic space action with pace, power and punch. Deceptively simple in the initial states leading to challenging finale.

This time you are Hal Bailman, potential saviour of the planet Farmel. Eight massive space fortresses are heading Farmel's way. As the deadline for disaster nears, Hal must destroy the fortresses. Each fortress consists of two sections: the approach – which takes place on an outerspace air base – and the fortress itself.

## WEAPONS

Hal is equipped with an unlimited supply of light blaster bullets. Later stages offer Hal the chance to acquire the more destructive crash beam bullets.

## SPECIALS

Hal starts with 3 lives which are lost when his energy reaches zero.

Therefore it is important to watch out for and collect the circled Es to keep strength up to a maximum. Circled Bs boost beams.

## THE ENEMY

A huge variety of space creeps.

## HINTS

**1** When in the air bases, look for + marks. Fly through them and they clear the screen of attackers.

**2** Barrier items – found only on the air bases – give Hal limited invincibility.

**3** Save energy by riding the lifts.

**4** Destroy the central reactor in each level to win.

**5** Remember the passwords at the end of games. These allow you to re-start the game at the same point.

**6** Rotating windows on the air bases sometimes contain Es and Bs. Take out the windows just in case.

## REMARKS

Air Fortress is a Shoot'em Up of the first degree, with ace action, sizzling sound and dynamic graphics.

## COMMENTS

PAUL: If Air Fortress takes your fancy it's worth investing in a joystick for maximum trigger-happy action.

THAT'S NICE: Almost pixel-perfect graphics.

THAT'S A SHAME: Poor plot scenario.

AIRWOLF™

| 8 | 8 | 7–70 | 1 |

## REVIEW

Television tie-in featuring the futuristic super-tech *Airwolf* helicopter. You are the hero pilot, Stringfellow Hawke, called out of retirement to rescue prisoners held at secret camps.

   This simulation puts you right in *Airwolf's* cockpit with a pilot's eye view out of the windscreen and of the gauges, message boards and radar. There are 20 missions to fly, and the game also features briefing officer Michael Goldsmith Briggs III and sidekick Santini, characters from the TV show.

## WEAPONS

Check-out *Airwolf*'s don't-mess-with-me hardware. It makes you square-jawed just reading it. There's computerized **satellite tracking**; a **30mm machine-gun**; heat-seeking **Copperhead missiles**; **night-flight controls**; **Doppler sensors** to spot hostile craft; automatic enemy **radar jam**.

## SPECIALS

The satellite-guided *Airwolf* **Indicator** holds the key to success. It pinpoints where your machine is in relation to enemy sites – airfields, prison camps and refuelling locations.

## THE ENEMY

Don't just think you can fly in and out rescuing prisoners without a hot reception. Air-to-air missiles, ground-to-air missiles and aircraft are at the enemy's disposal.

## HINTS

1 To make repairs, refuel or stock up with missiles – 15 of them – land at Refuelling Stations, marked by a barrel.
2 Enemy airfields are watched over by an airport control tower. Destroy them and the enemy will not be able to launch planes to you.
3 Prison sites are marked with a man holding his hands up in surrender. Position *Airwolf* tight above them before landing. The prisoner will then run to the helicopter.
4 You have to rescue all the prisoners from one level before you can move to the next.

## REMARKS

Learn to fly *Airwolf* so that it becomes second nature. If you can react automatically to a crisis without thinking, there is more chance of surviving.

## COMMENTS

PAUL: Top rate simulation, excellent fly-by-the-seat-of-your-pants action.

THAT'S NICE: A decent 'name' tie-in.

# ALL-PRO BASKETBALL™

|  8  |  7  | 7–70 | 1–2 |
|-----|-----|------|-----|

## REVIEW

All-action basketball thrill game which plays like the real thing and looks like a slick television sports show in which the camera switches from an overhead view of the court to close-ups of the players.

There are four combinations of play: Nintendo vs You; You vs Friend; You and Friend vs Nintendo; and Nintendo vs Nintendo, where the computer shows you what's what and puts everybody to shame.

## WEAPONS

Players can control passes, moves and shots. Each player has varying skills, for example, one player may be better at defence than attack.

## SPECIALS

Play closely follows the real rules of the game. Fouls are called for offences such as travelling, barging and foul shots.

## THE ENEMY

Players have a choice of 8 teams, with different playing characteristics.

## HINTS

**1** Learn the individual skills of your team. If you're winning, you may want to bring on an attacker to press home the advantage, or clamp down by bringing on a defender.
**2** Rest key players every so often.

## REMARKS

Super slick sports simulation, which might be helpful when working on strategies for real players?

## COMMENTS

JON: High energy action. Even Nigel improved the more he played!
THAT'S NICE: Half-time cheerleaders.
THAT'S A SHAME: Slightly ham-fisted controls. So that's why Nigel did so well!

# ANTICIPATION™

9    7–70    1–4

## REVIEW

An oddity among the range of Nintendo games, but no bad thing for all that. As the name implies, players must guess and spell out the name of an object being drawn on screen before the computer does. As the computer is actually doing the drawing, you may think this is a cheat. But the trusty Nintendo plays fair.

Guess correctly and a playing piece is moved round a track square by square. There are four colours, representing different groups of problems. There are 16 puzzle categories to choose from covering most of the general knowledge areas and there are 4 skill levels.

## WEAPONS

The mightiest weapon of all – your brain.

## SPECIALS

Make a mistake and you get one more crack before another player gets to go.

## THE ENEMY

The Nintendo and human rivals.

## HINTS

None, but your wits and the ability to visualize objects will see you through. The ability to spell will be a great help; watch out for Americanizations, though.

## REMARKS

Thoroughly entertaining party game, ideal for all ages, especially young gamesters.

## COMMENTS

PAUL: Branding a game educational can be the kiss of death. Anticipation manages to be entertaining and educational, especially for youngsters.

THAT'S NICE: A refreshing brain treat for tired Shoot'em Up freaks.

THAT'S A SHAME: Poor sound and effects.

16

7–70    1–2

## REVIEW

Bad Dudes with a good attitude go on a do-or-die mission to rescue the President of the USA from the hot hands of the Dragon Warriors. Martial arts mayhem rules!

Good conversion of the high kicking, punch 'n' jump, grab 'n' stab, throw 'n' blow it away coin-op. There are seven main playing areas to conquer, plenty of weapons for the Bad Dudes Blade and Striker to find. This is action with a capital 'A'.

## WEAPONS

Blade and Striker start with the ability to **kick, punch, jump** and **pick up** objects. Main weapons are **knives** and **nunchucks** (two sticks joined by a chain or rope).

## SPECIALS

**Special cans** restore energy. Remember 10 hits and 1 life is lost. Each level must be completed against the clock. Collect the **clocks** for extra seconds.

## THE ENEMY

*Blue, white, lady, dwarf,* red and flaming *ninjas, dogs, samurais* and *super-warriors.*

## HINTS

1  The City area is tough. Collect knives and nunchucks and watch out for the fire-shooting bald guy. He's hot stuff.

2  The big rig or lorry area. Keep on truckin'. Try and get to the front of the vehicle.

3  The sewer. A real brain drain.

4  Forest area. Can't see the mad dogs for the trees? You soon will. One's bite is worse than the other's bark.

5  The train area. Ride the rails. You're making tracks.

6  The cave. You're heading to the factory where the main man is held. Danger also comes from above. You'll get the point.

7  Factory area. Head for the lift and hopefully to a helicopter.

## REMARKS

Excellent action, good scene-setting, smooth scrolling.

## COMMENTS

NIGEL: Fight fans won't be disappointed. Keep ducking and diving to victory.

THAT'S NICE: Game play can continue after three lives are lost.

THAT'S A SHAME: Players have to take turns rather than play together.

BASES LOADED™

| 8 | 7 | 7–70 | 1–2 |

## REVIEW

Top-quality sports simulation, packed with detail and amazing playability – if you like baseball, that is. If not, these ball-park incidents will leave you cold. As with All-Pro Basketball, the visuals are very like telly coverage, with changing viewpoints and perspectives. All very slick.

There is a choice of 12 teams and 360 players, all with their talents and faults, top and fading form. The player's biorhythms are displayed. Everything, in fact, other than what he had for tea.

## WEAPONS

When pitching you can choose speed and position – high, inside, low and ourside. While batting, you can put emphasis on swinging high, low, stepping to and away from the pitcher. Fielders and runners can also be controlled.

## THE ENEMY

There are 12 teams, each made up of 30 players and that includes 12 pitchers. Each player has different statistics and batting averages which will alter their play.

## HINTS

Study the stats and teams to find out who are the in form players.

## REMARKS

Slick and smooth sports simulation. However, a certain familiarity with the rules, strategies of baseball is taken for granted.

## COMMENTS

PAUL: Whole new ball game – but only if you're a fan of baseball.
NIGEL: I prefer rounders!
THAT'S NICE: TV show presentation.
THAT'S A SHAME: Better instructions needed for non-US players.

### BATMAN™

   8       6     9–70    1

## REVIEW

This is the game-of-the-film-of-the-comic. Undeniably a shameless cash-in on the recent Batman film but also undeniably a superb game. It captures the dark, brooding and sinister atmosphere of the movie, although the game scenario is not particularly faithful to the film's plot. The Joker is on the rampage again in Gotham City. But you, as the caped crusader, must have the last laugh. To wipe the grin off the Joker's face, you must fight through 5 levels of pure platform action.

## WEAPONS

Each time Batman is touched by an enemy or hit by a weapon he loses energy. Let his 3 lives slip through your fingers and the game's over.

## THE ENEMY

After battling through each stage, Batman must confront the guardian before he can progress to the next level.

## HINTS

Well-placed body blows will defeat the 'guardians'.

## REMARKS

Superior animation and background graphics; tasty sound effects.

# COMMENTS

PAUL: There's nothing new about horizontally scrolling platform games but Batman is stylish enough to breathe new life into a jaded format. Mean, moody and – yes, I have to say it – magnificent.

THAT'S NICE: Cleverly animated game introduction.

THAT'S A SHAME: Pity there are no more than 5 levels.

## THE BATTLE OF OLYMPUS™

        7      7–16    1

## REVIEW

Adventure game set against a background firmly rooted in Greek mythology and set in the village of Elis in the region of Peloponnesus. Here, the lovely Helene lives with her lover Orpheus, until Helene dies from a snake bite – or so it seems.

Orpheus is told by Aphrodite that Helene is not really dead. Her soul is being held captive by Hades who wants to make her his queen. Our hero sets out to explore 8 lands, eventually reaching the land of Tartarus.

## WEAPONS

Orpheus ventures forth equipped with a **club**. Special magical items can be found to help his quest.

## SPECIALS

Magical items include the **Harp of Apollo**, the **Ocarina** – a musical instrument – the **Shield of Athena** and the **Bracelet of Power**.

## THE ENEMY

The entrance to Tartarus is guarded by *Cerberus*, a three-headed dog; *Lamia*, a vampire/serpent; half-man, half-horse, *Centaur*; the bull-headed *Minotaur*; the multi-headed *Hydra*; and the *Siren*, half-woman, half-bird.

## HINTS

1 Each land has a god or goddess which you must meet, including Zeus, Athena, Poseidon and Hermes. Each carries a useful item.

**2** The lands to explore are the Peloponnesus, Crete, Attica, Laconia, Phrygia, Argolis, Phthia and Tartarus.

## REMARKS

Not an adventure in the way most computer gamesters would understand, more an arcade adventure.

## COMMENTS

JON: It's a bit hit and myth.

THAT'S NICE: The Nintendo will call you by your name – providing you tell it in the first place.

THAT'S A SHAME: Graphics.

BAYOU BILLY™

6        4        7–70        1

## REVIEW

There's nothing like a swamp yomp, a waterlogged slog and bungle in the jungle to make you feel like a man. When the going gets rough, Bayou Billy gets tough. Bayou Billy! He sounds more like a strangled-voice bluegrass singer than a man with a mission. But Billy is no thick hick from Downtown, Nowhereville, USA.

And that mission is to rescue his gal Annabelle from the clutches of Mr Big who has kidnapped her and now faces a fate worse than having your Nintendo stolen. Yeah, the outlook is that bleak for Annabelle.

Bayou Billy must fight his way through three levels to cut Mr Big down to size. The battle starts in a swamp, changes to a road battle and finishes in Mr Big's jungle headquarters.

## WEAPONS

In the first section of the game, Bayou Billy starts with nothing more than his hands and feet to **punch** and **kick** Mr Big's cronies into tomorrow. Later he can pick up **sticks** and **knives**.

Survive and Billy finds some wheels. Slamming the hammer down, he roars off, two shotguns strapped to the hood and a grenade launcher on the roof. He needs them – Mr Big's boys attack him from cars and the air. Finally, he arrives at Mr Big's HQ. The action is now

Op. Wolf-style. Big's boys leap out. Luckily, Billy has an M–16 to persuade them to see the error of their ways. Or put big holes in them.

## SPECIALS

The main speciality is Billy – and you.

## THE ENEMY

They come on foot, by car, by air and out of the bushes, tough and terrible.

## HINTS

1 *Question*: What is the most dangerous and lethal plant in the world? *Answer*: The Am-bush. Remember that and there's hope for you and Billy.
2 In the last section you can use your Nintendo Light Zapper.
3 Take advantage of the practice modes for each level to hone your reactions and sharp-shooting.

## REMARKS

Taken individually, the three sections of this game – Double Dragon, Road Blaster and Operation Wolf – are highly derivative. Put them together and you've got a very enjoyable game, providing you don't have any of the games they're based on.

## COMMENTS

PAUL: Very playable but lacking top-notch graphics and sound. Not quite a master-blaster but worthy of anybody's time – and perhaps money?
THAT'S NICE: Another Light Zapper game.
THAT'S A SHAME: Lacks originality.

BIONIC COMMANDO™

8     6     7–17     1

## REVIEW

Don't mess with Super Joe, he's a one-man arm-y. One of his arms contains more than skin, muscle and bone, but more of that later.

Things are grim: invaders are marauding across the country, the army is destroyed. Things can't get much worse, but the boffins have come to the rescue – by creating a bionic army, turning ordinary Joe into Super Joe. Invaders, watch out. There are 20 zones of all-out action coming up. The first 12 are battle scenes. The rest are neutral zones where you can get supplies and ask questions.

## WEAPONS

Super Joe sets out with his **bionic arm**, **rifle** and **communicator**. His amazing arm is 10ft long and he can use it to swing through the trees, leaving the enemy stunned. Other weapons he can use are a **short-range gun** which sprays lethal lead, an armour and building-piercing **rocket gun**, **three-way gun**, a **hyper-bazooka** and a **flare bomb**.

## SPECIALS

Kill an enemy and you get a **bullet**. A **charm** blocks one bullet, a **bulletproof vest** gives you protection against two bullets, while a **helmet** protects against three bullets. **Communicators** receive messages from HQ. **Iron boots** will give you a kick. **Medicine** restores energy and a **permit** allows access to neutral zones. **POW** is a ball of power which gives you limited protection.

## THE ENEMY

The enemy comes in all shapes and forms, equipped with a formidable array of hardware – rifles, bazookas, cannons, laser cannons, helicopters and jeeps. To destroy the helicopter shoot through its window as you dive off the ledge. You lose one of your three lives.

## HINTS

1 Make use of the map. When moving to a new zone, you don't have to follow game prompts.
2 Use your bionic arm to keep the enemy at arm's length, besides reaching and swinging.
3 Pick up the flares in Area 13. They will come in useful.
4 To get out of a level during a fight, hold the start button and push the 'A' & 'B' buttons together.

## REMARKS

Nice variation on the army Shoot'em Up. Excellent graphics, super sound and completely addictive game play.

## COMMENTS

PAUL: If you like this type of Shoot'em Up, you'll be hard-pressed to find a better one.

JON: You know I love 'em!

THAT'S NICE: The bionic arm is a good, and useful, gimmick.

THAT'S A SHAME: Instructions are a little odd. Press the 'A' button to fire guns and extend the bionic arm.

## BLADES OF STEEL™

| 7 | 5 | 6–20 | 1–2 |
|---|---|------|-----|

## REVIEW

The setting for this game is no hack and slay killing floor for muscle-bound, loincloth-clad barbarians. The warriors in this arena are armed with jolly hockey sticks. Tough players, eight teams, face-offs, penalties, checking, fights, exhibition matches, tournaments, variable skills (junior, college, professional) – hockey is one of the roughest, toughest sports going!

## WEAPONS

**Sticks** and **blades**. But these aren't weapons – not officially, of course.

## SPECIALS

You will be penalized for shooting the length of the rink, slashing and checking. If you are playing this rough, do not be surprised if fists fly and somebody ends up in the sin bin.

## THE ENEMY

No enemy. We're all good sports. Aren't we?

## HINTS

1 Keep an eye on the flashing arrow. This indicates where a shot or pass will go.

2 Line the goalie up with the arrow. This cuts down goal chances.

## REMARKS

Pity about the use of flashing to indicate the player who is being controlled.

## COMMENTS

NIGEL: I suspect the flickering graphics are a trade-off for speed, but I can live with that. Excellent action. If you're not into sports this game would be a frozen waste. For those who are, it's rinky-dink.

THAT'S NICE: Despite minor quibbles about graphics and sound, the overall game is a winner.

THAT'S A SHAME: Dodgy sound effects.

### BLASTER MASTER™

6 6 7–70 1

## REVIEW

The lesson of Blaster Master is simple: take care where you dump radioactive waste. Not only does it turn your pet frog into a huge mutant, it also addles the brain and makes people come up with bizzare game scenarios.

In this one, the frog mutates after bumping into a radioactive chest which has been carelessly left in your garden. It then disappears down a hole and you follow because, for some reason beyond comprehension, you would like this giant – and probably highly toxic – frog back. If things sound a little unhinged so far, just wait! You next find yourself in a subterranean radioactive world, heaving with mutants and controlled by the sinister Plutonium Boss.

And what a stroke of luck. There's a handy tank/armoured vehicle for you to use exploring. Most of the game's 8 stages can be explored by staying in this highly mobile tank, but for some you have to leave the tank and investigate on foot.

## WEAPONS

Besides the **tank**, there are also **gun capsules** to boost ammo supplies and **power capsules** to boost your lift force.

25

## SPECIALS

Each level also contains some heavy hardware to be found and used on the mutant creatures. A **super-cannon**, a **wall-crusher**, a **capsule** which allows you to hover, **keys**, **capsules** which help you dive, climb walls and ceilings, a **homing missile**, a **multi-warhead missile**, and a **Thunder Break** – this last generates an electromagnetic pulse of lightning.

## THE ENEMY

The main enemies are the *mutant bosses* who control the exit to each level. They are big, mean and ugly. As each one is destroyed you will be rewarded with weapons. The exit to the final level is controlled by two main mutants – a horrid *clawed creature* and the *Plutonium Boss* himself.

## HINTS

1 A life is lost when you run out of power. Keep topping up your life force with power capsules.
2 Watch out for landmines.
3 Study the maps provided, and know where you are and where you are going. This can help when the pressure starts.
4 Practice jumping.

## REMARKS

Generally ace graphics, animation and decent sound track and effects.

## COMMENTS

PAUL: The theme of Blaster Master is utterly stupid, one of the worst I've come across.
JON: If I'd only read about the game, I wouldn't have given it a second thought.
NIGEL: The game is rescued by excellent playability. Check it out.
THAT'S NICE: Good sound track gives the game extra pace.
THAT'S A SHAME: Stupid plot.

# BUBBLE BOBBLE™

| 6 | 6 | 6–60 | 1–2 |

## REVIEW

It's time to monster mash the beastie boys in a prehistoric maze rave. Enter the cutest, tail-wagging dinosaurs you're ever likely to meet this side of extinction – Bob and Bub.

Baron von Blubba is the evil prince of Whales, a mean-minded mammal who has kidnapped two of Bob and Bub's friends. And our heroes aren't going to sit idly by twiddling their tails and let him get away with it! They decide to rescue their friends by battling through 2 worlds. Easy? Not when you know there are more than 100 monster-packed levels to get through!

## WEAPONS

The only weapons Bob and Bub have all the time – apart from your quick wits and reactions – are **magic bubbles** which trap the monsters. If our heroes can burst the bubble the monster inside changes into a bonus prize. Each level must be cleared of monsters before you can move on to the next.

Watch out for secret weapons. There are at least 14 different types. Here are a few: the **bomb** will clear all the monsters from the screen; **Candy** enables Bob and Bub to blow better bubbles; **Magic Jar** gives access to a bonus round; **umbrellas** can help you jump 5 levels.

## SPECIALS

Every so often, a letter from the word 'Extend' will float down the screen. Capture it. Collect all the letters in the word and you can skip a level.

## THE ENEMY

The big baddie is *Baron von Blubba*. Watch out – he will step in if you're too slow. Then there's *Beluga*, who sounds like caviar but this whale is an easy catch. Also watch out for hip-hopping *Coiley*, the red-hot *Incendo* and the aptly named *Bubble Buster*.

## HINTS

1 Although you can get through Bubble Bobble on your own, it is

27

helpful to play with a friend. Working as a team makes it easier to gang up on the monsters.

2 Learn to ride the bubbles. A gentle hop will see Bob or Bub surfing on them. This can make it easier to capture monsters.

3 Burst bubbles in bunches to boost points.

4 Experiment with your 5-letter passwords. Different combinations of letters will give access to different screens.

5 It's often a good idea to let the monsters come to you rather than chasing after them.

6 The Crystal Ball in level 99 is essential to further progress.

## REMARKS

Playing either with or against a friend adds interest and fun.

## COMMENTS

PAUL: Superb value for money, excellent playability and enduring popularity. Getting into bubble trouble is recommended.

THAT'S NICE: Cute characters – the stuff sequels are made of.

THAT'S A SHAME: The maze-style games lead to repetitive play.

BUMP 'N' JUMP™

   7       7      7–70     1

## REVIEW

The Day of the Jackals has arrived. They're a rock-hard road racing gang who have kidnapped your girlfriend, Bunny. You're off in hot pursuit in a super mean machine over 16 courses.

But the highway isn't just used by you and the Jackals. Ordinary folk are riding the tarmac in lorries, bulldozers and cement mixers all with, it seems, unsafe loads. Things just keep dropping off and getting in your way.

## WEAPONS

Your car can bump rivals off the road, earning points, and jump over cars, obstacles and hazards.

## SPECIALS

You start with 3 lives and 100 litres of **motion lotion**. Watch out for extra lives, and find **power barrels** with more go-go juice.

## THE ENEMY

These divide into two groups – the real bad guys, the *Jackals*, and the others who are not really bad but get in your way: *police cars*, *ambulances*, *bulldozers*, *cement mixers*, *fuel tankers* and *sand lorries*. Other hazards on the roads include *oil*, *sand* and *concrete*.

Watch out for the *Dark Jackal* – he's the leader. The other gang members ride in jeeps and buggies.

## HINTS

1 You must be driving at around 95 mph to be able to jump.
2 If forced off the road, try a jump. It may get you out of trouble.
3 Watch for red warning signs by the road.
4 Don't follow lorries for long. You never know what's going to fall off the back and get in your way.
5 Seek out the hidden repair stations.
6 Always grab power barrels when you can.

## REMARKS

Good, exciting action, but graphics and sound are not really up to normal Nintendo quality.

## COMMENTS

JON: Young gamers will probably like Bump 'n' Jump best.
THAT'S NICE: Easy driving controls.
THAT'S A SHAME: Poor value.

### CALIFORNIA GAMES™

| 7 | 6 | 7–17 | 1–8 |

## REVIEW

Stick on a Beach Boys tape and get set for six screwball sports from the land of sun, sea, sand and we'll have fun, fun, fun.

## WEAPONS

No weapons, just your skill.

## SPECIALS

The action covers many things. **BMX bike racing** takes on the hazards of holes, rocks, water and still wins. Try some wheelies. **Chucking the frisbee** and catching it. **Rollerskating** – cover the course avoiding cracks, piles of sand, beach balls and bananas. **Surfing** – ride the waves, turn tricks and win points – but it ain't easy. **Half-pipe skateboarding** – perform stunts – hand plants, kick and aerial turns – against the clock in half a concrete tube. Dangerous! The **foot bag** is totally bizarre: juggling a bag with your feet to perform 11 fancy tricks.

## THE ENEMY

The *computer* or anybody you can get to play.

## HINTS

Success depends on joystick dexterity. Practice, practice, practice.

## REMARKS

Mastering these will take a lot of effort and the fun you'll get from California Games will depend on how quickly that takes you.

## COMMENTS

PAUL: Can't say I'm that impressed with the screwball sports. I know it's a big success but its attraction passes me by.

JON: California Lames more like!

THAT'S NICE: Good for youngsters.

THAT'S A SHAME: Poor graphics.

## CASTLEVANIA II: SIMON'S QUEST™

9     8–70     1

## REVIEW

The sequel to Castlevania, in which vampire hunter Simon Belmont finds that he bears the curse of Dracula. If you have played the first

30

game, you will know Simon had to make sure Dracula was out for the count.

Simon's only hope is to get the curse lifted by returning to Castlevania, finding the 5 parts of big D's dismembered body and destroying him once and for all. (Or at least until Nintendo thinks it would be a great idea to make Castlevania III.)

## WEAPONS

Simon starts the game with a **whip** but as he – or rather you – gain more experience, more powerful weapons can be bought. For instance, **holy water, garlic, fire, daggers** etc.

## SPECIALS

Mysteries can be seen through **Dracula's eyeball**, if you get a grip on it.

## THE ENEMY

*Monsters*, *zombies*, *vampire bats* and, of course, *Dracula*. There are ordinary locals scattered around the game who might help or hinder your quest.

## HINTS

1 Draw a map of the village, town, swamp, cemetery and mansion.
2 To buy an object you must defeat several monsters, gaining hearts which can be swapped for weapons.
3 Holy water is useful in defeating most monsters, uncovering objects or discovering traps.
4 Empty rooms sometimes contain hidden secrets.
5 Find the invisible staircases.

## REMARKS

Superb adventure, in places fiendishly difficult, reeking in ghoulish atmosphere. It also contains enough arcade action to satisfy dedicated zappers.

## COMMENTS

NIGEL: Hugely enjoyable, superbly produced and well-designed variation on the rather hackneyed vampire theme.
THAT'S NICE: Brilliant graphics.
THAT'S A SHAME: Little sound and no map provided.

# CITY CONNECTION™

6–16    1–2

## REVIEW

City Connection is a game where you really get to paint the town. You take the part of a petty crook who has broken into a paint store in New York City and stolen leaking cans of paint. As you drive away, the paint drips all over the highway. Not surprisingly, the police are soon onto you and follow your trail through 6 world cities. To get from one city to another you must completely cover the roads with paint.

## WEAPONS

Your **skill at driving** is the main weapon with which you can escape going to gaol. Your car can also jump. There are **oil cans** around which you can toss on to the road in front of the cop cars.

## SPECIALS

Watch for and collect the **balloons** which allow you to warp to other levels.

## THE ENEMY

The long arm of the law.

## HINTS

1 Try not to hit a police car, squash cats or smash into roadblocks as this will lose you a life.
2 If it looks like you are going to crash, try and jump the obstacle.
3 You need three balloons to warp levels.

## REMARKS

Simple game which is hard to play, competent sound and vision, but the totally stupid game scenario somehow makes it unappealing.

## COMMENTS

PAUL: Lacks any sort of grabability. Don't think it will become a cult game like some do, the challenge doesn't seem really worthwhile.

THAT'S NICE: Some good sound effects.
THAT'S A SHAME: Slight flicker on some of the cars.

## CLASH AT DEMONHEAD™

7      6      7–70      1

## REVIEW

A slightly odd combination of Shoot'em Up with adventure overtones. Clash at Demonhead sees secret agent Bang on a mission to rescue Professor Plum who is being forced to build a doomsday weapon. There are around 30 different routes to complete the game and 2 ways of winning. Either stop the Professor building the bomb, or if that's already happened, you must defuse it. To get to the end of the game you must also collect a set of medallions.

## WEAPONS

Bang must earn dosh to buy weapons. If he has enough he can go to the weapon mart for some heavy duty shopping. Special weapons include **aqualungs**, a **protective suit** which allows Bang to walk on lava, **super-boots** and a **jet pack**.

## SPECIALS

Take a look under the water and lava, but wear the right gear.

## THE ENEMY

Bad dudes include a *skeletal law-breaker*, *deadly pandas*, a *motorbike-riding lizard* and a *guy who breaks off pieces from his body* and uses them as bombs.

## HINTS

1 Find apples and hearts to increase energy and life-force.
2 Gold can be converted to money for shopping.
3 There are secret passages between some routes. Some routes are one-way only.
4 Never run out of money.

## REMARKS

An odd game but extremely playable; action and adventure all the way, constantly challenging. Excellent graphics and sound, too.

## COMMENTS

PAUL: Because there are various ways to win you can play this game over and over again.

JON: There's always something new to see, do and buy.

NIGEL: Clash at Demonhead maintains its playability for a long time.

THAT'S NICE: Imaginative game concept.

THAT'S A SHAME: The only shame is on you if this game is not in your collection.

COBRA TRIANGLE™

   6        5       6–16      1

## REVIEW

Not a deadly duel with a snake-eyed enemy, but a water-borne race against the clock. The Cobra of the title is, in fact, a Cobra Class speed boat. There are 8 levels of increasingly difficult play. As you race the river, you must collect pods, dodge or destroy mines, kill monsters, shoot targets and jump waterfalls.

## WEAPONS

**Pods** can be collected to increase speed, missiles, firepower and force field.

## THE ENEMY

Anybody and everybody that gets in your way. Take 'em out, fast!

## HINTS

The most difficult part is jumping the waterfall. Make sure you have full power before trying it.

## REMARKS

So-so race'em, blast'em game. Okay graphics and sound but nothing to get worked up about.

## COMMENTS

NIGEL: Each level is fairly repetitive and interest is only really maintained by the increasing difficulty.

THAT'S NICE: Nice Cobra control.

THAT'S A SHAME: Repetitive.

CONTRA™

   8      6    7–20   1–2

## REVIEW

For no nonsense, pulse-pounding action Shoot'em Ups, you can't get much better than Contra. It's a coin-op classic, a home computer smash and now it's taking the Nintendo by storm. Contra is better known as Gryzor. For some reason the name has changed on Nintendo, but otherwise the game remains the same.

A huge alien attack craft has crashed into the earth. The leader of the aliens, Red Falcon, has plans for world domination. Enter those all-American super-troopers Lance and Bill whose aim is to penetrate the craft and wipe out Red Falcon and the alien menace. There are 8 alien-packed levels for our two heroes to battle through.

## WEAPONS

You start out with a more-or-less standard weapon. Taking out gun emplacements may expose bonus icons. These allow weapons to be upgraded. My favourite is the rapid-five **three-way gun**, dealing death and destruction, and providing such a vicious onslaught you can move through the level quite quickly.

## SPECIALS

**Smart-bomb**. It provides mass-destruction. Use it carefully.

## THE ENEMY

Rough, tough and they don't give up.

## HINTS

1 Shooting skills are paramount. Make every shot count.

2 On the first level, when trying to take out gun emplacements, it's

35

best to move in, aim, fire and withdraw. Stand still and you're an easy target.

## REMARKS
Quality shows and Contra is quality. It scores in all departments – graphics, sound and playability.

## COMMENTS
PAUL: There are good games, great games and brilliant games. Contra is brilliant. If you want what is probably the best Blast'em Up available, then buy this one.
JON: Brilliant!
THAT'S NICE: Very tough game play means you'll keep on playing.
THAT'S A SHAME: Ain't no shame. It's great.

CYBERNOID™

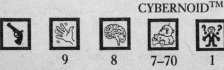

| 9 | 8 | 7–70 | 1 |

## REVIEW
As test-pilot for The Federation's new Cybernoid space-fighter, you're despatched on a mission to rid three storage asteroids – filled with rare minerals or valuable gems – of space pirates known as Zogs. A simple storyline, simply told, but hard to actually achieve. You're given a choice of easy, hard and lethal levels and 9 lives to start exploring the 3 levels, each with around 50 rooms.

## WEAPONS
Your ship is equipped with a basic **laser blaster** with everlasting power.

## SPECIALS
Other weapons can be found. These have limited power but can be replenished. Watch out for **bombs, bouncers**, which will take out anything; **genocide missiles** will take out all Zogs on screen and, unfortunately, some useful items; **radar-controlled missiles**; a **shield** which gives limited protection.

There are also two other weapons which can be attached to the Cybernoid – a **rear blaster** and a **cybermace**, a power weapon which circles your craft wiping out everything.

## THE ENEMY

You rack up points for wiping out the various *Zogs* and items such as *Zoggian missiles*.

## HINTS

1 Keep an eye on time. It's limited.
2 Brute force will not always see you through. Delicate control of the Cybernoid combined with precise timing will be needed to penetrate some parts of the game.

## REMARKS

Cybernoid is a game of the highest quality, maintaining the highest tradition of space Shoot'em Ups. It has solid programming, above average sound and vision, and is totally addictive.

## COMMENTS

JON: Classic space action, deadly difficult to master, vastly entertaining and challenging.
PAUL: A must.
THAT'S NICE: Everything.
THAT'S A SHAME: Weak storyline – but that really doesn't matter.

### DESERT COMMANDER™

| | 5 | 9 | 10–60 | 1–2 |

## REVIEW

There are 5 battle scenarios set in North Africa in the Second World War, but the sides are specified so you choose who you want to be. The scenarios are First Battle, Way to Victory, Offence and Defence, Bloody Battle and North African Front. Players cannot increase the number of units they have but they can trade one type of unit for another – armoured cars for tanks, for instance.

## WEAPONS

Ground and air units are **anti-aircraft gun**, **bomber**, **armoured car**, **mobile troop carrier**, **field cannon**, **fighter**, **infantry**, **supply truck**, **tank**, **troop transport** and **headquarters**.

## SPECIALS

The battle commands are: **power**, a unit status report; **movement**, the ability to move units with cursor keys; **attack**, again the units moved with the cursor.

## THE ENEMY

Unknown, but as this is North Africa during the Second World War, probably British or German.

## HINTS

Each gamester will play this game differently so it's up to you to work out individual strategies. If they work, keep them to yourself.

## REMARKS

As far as is known, Desert Commander is Nintendo's only war simulation. As with most simulations, the graphics and sound are not really important.

## COMMENTS

PAUL: Fairly playable but unsatisfactory. Why aren't the sides named? Half the interest in war simulations is seeing if you can re-write history.

THAT'S NICE: Nice battle themes.

THAT'S A SHAME: No background.

DONKEY KONG,™   DONKEY KONG JUN,™   DONKEY KONG MATH,™   DONKEY KONG II™

| 5 | 5 | 7–17 | 1–2 |

## REVIEW

Along with Mario Bros., Donkey Kong was the first smash for Nintendo in the early eighties. Time, and rapidly increasing programming standards and increased player expectation have meant the game has not lasted particularly well.

**Donkey Kong.** Four screens of really ancient platform and ladder action. You must rescue Mario's girlfriend from the clutches of an

38

enormous ape who insists on chucking barrels at you. Undeniably a classic, but it doesn't stand the test of time.

**Donkey Kong Jnr**. More monkey business – again over four screens – in which you must rescue your father from Mario's prison. Undeniably not a classic. More a cash-in. Forget it.

**Donkey Kong Math**. This is supposed to be educational. Warn your teacher. It's something some schools might be silly enough to waste money on. For 'educational' read 'boring'.

**Donkey Kong II**. Donkey Kong goes ape again – badly. And only over three screens! Forget it.

## HINTS

A couple of hours and you'll have the games sussed!

## REMARKS

These are for nostalgia freaks only. All our yesterplays.

## COMMENTS

PAUL: Save your pennies for something else which offers longer-lasting playability.

THAT'S NICE: It has a place in history.

THAT'S A SHAME: Flogging a dead donkey.

### DOUBLE DRAGON™

7      5      7–70             1–2

## REVIEW

Enter the dragon in the form of high-kicking, power-punching Billy Lee. The game opens with a gang of thugs – the Black Warriors – punching Billy Lee's girl in the stomach and then carrying her away.

Billy sets out on a trail of revenge, leaving corpses to the left and right. This game is very violent. As the carnage increases so does Billy's score, earning extra 'hearts'. With each heart he acquires more deadly skills at karate and judo.

In two-player mode, Billy is joined in this orgy of violence by brother Jimmy.

## WEAPONS

**Knives, baseball bats, whips** and **dynamite**. They can be used by Billy – and on him. Billy can also **kick, punch, jump, head butt**, throw and **use his elbows** to deadly effect.

## SPECIALS

There are two special moves from which the street gangs do not recover. First, there is the extremely nasty **hair-pull** and knee to the face. Also **pinning the enemy down** and punching the face.

## THE ENEMY

A variety of mean street punks and evil mutants. They are *Abobo*, a muscleman with access to bombs; *Linda*, a punchy lady with a whip; *Lopar*, oil-drum-chucking lout; *Williams*, armed with bat or knife; and *Willy*, the machinegun-toting Big Boss. Not the sort of people you would want to meet in a dark alley!

## HINTS

**1** If possible, always get a weapon. It increases your chances of survival.
**2** Don't rush straight into the attack. Lure them to you and try a surprise kick.

## REMARKS

Is violence a suitable subject for games? Lots of games contain violence – against space ships, aliens, cars etc. This is realistic violence by people against people and as such might be thought unsuitable. Films that contain severe violence normally have viewing restrictions. Perhaps each game should be given a certificate?

## COMMENTS

JON: Providing you do not object to the extreme violence in Double Dragon – and this is one of the most violent games around – it is extremely well done. The top class graphics make it chillingly realistic. It's a classic.
THAT'S NICE: Tough, lasting action.
THAT'S A SHAME: A few annoying bugs.

# DOUBLE DRAGON II: THE REVENGE™

  6          5          7–70                    1–2

## REVIEW

Billy and Jimmy Lee are back again this time in a futuristic gang warfare set in a nuclear-ravaged New York City. Boy, is it still tough on the streets!

The Black Shadow Warrior, punks, freaks and criminals, are trying to take over the street. Once again Billy's girlfriend is having a tough time. This time she's been gunned down. Mightily miffed, Billy is out for revenge. It's carnage time again.

There are several player combinations: Billy vs the punks, Billy and Jimmy vs the punks and Billy vs Jimmy vs the punks. There are also 3 difficulty levels: practice, warrior and supreme master.

## WEAPONS

Besides skills in the martial arts, Billy can also make use of **guns, knives, chains, firebombs, sticks** and a **boomerang**.

## SPECIALS

In the supreme master level there are 9 missions. The fight action rages in the gang's HQ, a helicopter, an underwater base, a forest, a dungeon, a mission where you fight baddies looking like you. Only then do you reach the final confrontation.

## THE ENEMY

An unholy alliance of misfits, freaks and flakes who take no lip and deal in death.

## HINTS

Playing by yourself is tough. Ask a friend to fight alongside you and you will go a long way.

## REMARKS

A worthy sequel that includes all the best of Double Dragon with some new features.

# COMMENTS

PAUL: Excellent action.

THAT'S NICE: Pixel perfect animation – well, almost.

THAT'S A SHAME: The sense of guilt which comes from enjoying the violence.

DOUBLE DRIBBLE™

| 7 | 6 | 6–60 | 1–2 |

## REVIEW

The name of the game is basketball. Four teams, four periods of play and a time limit – those are the vital ingredients of DD.

## WEAPONS

Pure paddle-pounding skill.

## SPECIALS

There are three ways to score baskets. First, a **throw within the boundary**. Secondly, the **out of boundary play** and, thirdly, the **slam dunk** – smashing the ball into the basket from above.

## THE ENEMY

The teams to choose from are *Chicago*, *New York*, *Boston* and *Los Angeles*.

## HINTS

Practise, practise, practise.

## REMARKS

Nice introduction to basketball, easy to get going, uncomplicated rules. The emphasis is on action rather than strategy.

## COMMENTS

NIGEL: Double Dribble is tasty without being mouth-watering. A game that will maintain its appeal.

THAT'S NICE: Simple play, easy to master.

THAT'S A SHAME: Players lack detail.

# DUCK HUNT™

6     2     6–60     1–2

## REVIEW

The hunt is on. Your faithful old hound dog flushes out the ducks for you to take pop shots at. You can choose whether to have one or two of our feathered friends flapping left to right across the screen, but you only have three shots to down them. Just parting their feathers is not good enough – you have to bring them down to earn points. Miss, and your faithful old duck dog shows his true colours and laughs at you.

Duck Hunt is an extremely simple game, but it is also extremely playable. Once you get your eye in and start bagging the blighters, the ducks start flapping even faster across the screen. When your aim is so accurate that the ducks don't stand a chance, invite a friend to control the birds. It spices up the game.

If you get fed up with the ducks, try the extra Clay Pigeon Shooting game. In this you have to hit the clays before they disappear from sight.

## WEAPONS

The **NES Light Zapper**.

## THE ENEMY

*Ducks*. Lots of them. Luckily, they don't shoot back!

## HINTS

Practice makes perfect. If you're incapable of shooting straight, try another game.

## REMARKS

Using the Zapper makes the game. For added realism, arrange all your pot plants along the top of your sofa and then crouch behind it, springing up and down to shoot at the ducks. A faithful dog by your side also adds to the excitement. If you haven't a dog, try a cat.

## COMMENTS

PAUL: Initially exciting, but the repetitive play quickly leads to boredom.

JON: Very poor taste. Why encourage blood sports in the basic pack?
NIGEL: Highly distasteful!
THAT'S NICE: The Light Zapper.
THAT'S A SHAME: Limited play.

## DUCK TALES™

4      4      5–11      1

## REVIEW

Licensed from Walt Disney, the game has Scrooge going on a quest for hidden treasure in 5 exotic locations. His nephews Huey, Dewey and Louis, plus other characters from the cartoon shows, make an appearance. There are 3 levels of difficulty, but they are all easy and designed for the youngest of gamesters.

## SPECIALS

The locations and treasures are **Amazon jungle** (Sceptre of Zarduck), **Africa** (Giant Diamond), **Himalayas** (Crown of Genghis Khan), **The Moon** (Green Cheese of Longevity) and **Duckburg**).

## REMARKS

Strictly for youngsters and Walt Disney fans.

## COMMENTS

PAUL: A good present for a younger brother or sister.
THAT'S NICE: Cute characters.
THAT'S A SHAME: For what it is, there's nothing wrong with it.

## EIGHT EYES™

7      6      7–70      1–2

## REVIEW

Great game in which you control both a super-fighter, Orin, and an attack falcon called Cutrus. The world is just recovering from a nuke war and is under the thumb of the 8 eyes (jewels that protect the earth). They've been stolen by the 8 Dukes. You've gotta gettem back, gettit?

44

## WEAPONS

Terrific super-duper **attack falcon**, otherwise your trusty **sword**. Stand well back and slash. Get too close and you'll be damaged. Other great weapons include a **boomerang**, a **dagger**, a **gun**, an **ice ball**, a **molotov cocktail** and a **power ball**.

## SPECIALS

When you kill a Duke, he leaves a **jewel** behind. Touch it and it will reveal a **password**.

## THE ENEMY

There are 8 worlds, each with their own peculiar bad guys. Africa is the home of *King Amin*. He fights with a gigantic axe, which he sometimes throws. The Arabian, *Rashal*, is a knife thrower. The sorceror of *Tanatos* blasts with fire balls. The Nazi *Walter*, a German stereotype, chucks swastikas in Germany. The vanishing *Nasim* of India will bug the life out of you! The Italian bad guy *Geno* fights with a steel-tipped playing card (why?). *Bartona* the Spaniard is a fencer, while the final challenge is the whip-wielding *Ruth*.

## HINTS

1 The jewel in Africa is called the Devil of Zimbabwe, an orange topaz.

2 The Arabian jewel is a white diamond called the Tear of the Nile.

3 The Egyptian jewel is a red ruby called the Blood of Tutankhamen.

4 In Germany the Fairy of Granada is a purple amethyst.

5 The Indian yellow obsidian is called the Wing of Angels.

6 The Italian green emerald is the Dancing Princess of Frenelia.

7 The Black Pearl from Spain is called the Black Butterfly of Pereshusu.

8 The House of Ruth has a blue diamond called the Nail of Satan.

9 Try one of the European countries as your first target.

10 Begin your game with Spain, then Egypt.

11 No more clues, but finish up in Arabia!

12 Grab the white crosses for power-ups.

13 Power-ups include Blue Jars, C jars, G jars, S jars and Z jars. Hit them to get power.

## REMARKS

Tricky in places. Not a bad game really.

## EXCITEBIKE™

6    5    6–60    1–2

## REVIEW

Horizontally-scrolling race track action against opponents and against the clock, while dodging obstacles.

PAUL: Simple idea, not stunning graphically but extremely entertaining.

## FIST OF THE NORTH STAR™

8    6    6–60    1

## REVIEW

If you want tough bare fist combat, then Fist of the North Star is worth checking out. Not much originality in the plot – the hero, expert in the art of Gento Karate, takes on the henchmen of the evil Emperor Heaven to rescue the citizens of the Central Imperial capital. Gento Karate is the specialized art of becoming transparent so enemies and objects can pass straight through you.

The screen-displays to keep an eye on are the power meter – full power being seven stars (see Specials) – the bomb meter and the normal energy meter.

## WEAPONS

The 8 main opponents start out using **bare fists,** but later resort to **fire balls, light bombs, sliding kicks, claws** and **smokeballs.**

## SPECIALS

Watch out for the **Flag of Hokuto** which restores the hero's energy. There are other objects to look out for as well. **Stars** are often found when an enemy is KO-ed: an open star can boost your strength by four times and a solid star can increase it by five to seven times. **Shooting power** is available after 20 bad guys have been killed. **Yulia's necklace** also comes in two versions – the silver one restores shooting power while the gold allows you access to the mysteries of Gento Karate.

## THE ENEMY

*Bask*, whose main weapons are Kazan Prison and clenching claws. *Gayler* uses smokeballs and fireballs as his main weapons, but he can also spin illusions. *Tiger* has light bombs and deadly kicks. *Solia* uses special armour. *Blue Light Bolts* can throw three light bombs at once. *Red Light Bronza* has light bombs and, more terrifying, Gento Karate. *Gold Falco* uses light bombs, Gento Karate and sliding kicks. *Shula* practises the sliding kick.

## HINTS

1 Watch out for false game-ending on level 7. Press Continue.
2 If you can collect a full quota of stars, you will be almost unbeatable.
3 Kicks will deal with most of the early enemies.
4 Exits from one screen to another are not always obvious. Check behind things.

## REMARKS

Standard Bash'em Up format which has nothing desperately original to recommend it – except its playability.

## COMMENTS

PAUL: Well put together, nicely programmed, but fails to capture the imagination.
THAT'S NICE: Quick control response.
THAT'S A SHAME: Lacks original thought.

FLYING DRAGON: THE SECRET SCROLL™

  7        6        7–70       1

## REVIEW

Hiryu-no-Ken is, apparently, the ultimate kung-fu stance. Master it and nobody is likely to call you a wimp. But disaster has struck. The Secret Scolls of Hiryu-no-Ken, written by martial arts expert Juan, have been stolen.

You, as Ryhui, a pupil of Juan, discover that one scroll was not stolen. It has been given to Gengai, the bishop of Shorinji. Ryhui, in time, becomes the representative of Shorinji in the World Tournament of Contact Sports. He must play against the beastly Tusk Soldiers who are behind the theft of the Hiryu-no-Ken scrolls.

What may at first appear to be a simple tale of another hero hitting the martial arts revenge trail is, in fact, a little more complex. To get the most from this game you must train to perfect your fighting skills. At certain points, the game halts for a martial arts lesson. During the game you must fight various opponents at various contact sports and if you triumph, they will be unmasked as the Tusk Soldiers and a scroll will be recovered.

## WEAPONS

The six events in the World Tournament of Contact Sports are boxing, karate, kick-boxing, kung-fu, martial arts and wrestling. There are many kicks and punches to develop but they will require practice. They include the **cyclone kick**, the **middle kick** and the **spinning ground kick**. Other special items can be found to boost jumping and kicking power – and points.

## SPECIALS

There are three: **Hiryu-no-Ken,** a powerful mid-air spinning kick; **saucer,** that packs a powerful blow; and **throw,** in which you use the enemy's power against him and throw him over your shoulder.

## THE ENEMY

Destroy a group of *Tusk Soldiers* and you will then face the *Tusk Beast* to recover the scroll. Destroy the dragon statues to discover hidden items.

## HINTS

1 As they are recovered, the scrolls will enhance Ryhui's power and skills.
2 Scroll One increases attacking power.
3 Scroll Two increases speed.
4 Scroll Three allows you to practise the art of Hiryu-no-Ken more frequently without huge drains on energy.
5 Scroll Four develops jumping power.
6 Scroll Five boosts defence power.

## REMARKS

Nice variation on the kick and punch style of game. The ability to develop martial arts skills means there is always something new to do or, at least, to perfect.

## COMMENTS

JON: Smash'em Up sports simulation with adventure overtones. It's got a lot to offer.
THAT'S NICE: Hidden features.
THAT'S A SHAME: No two-player mode.

## FRIDAY THE 13TH™

6      6      7–70      1

## REVIEW

Axe-wielding film monster Jason breaks free from celluloid land and runs amok in your Nintendo. Just keep yourself alive . . .

Fans of the Friday the 13th films will know what to expect with this gore-soaked offering – mega violence in the worst possible taste. You are one of 6 counsellors looking after 15 teenagers at Crystal Lake, a task made more difficult by the mad Jason who is marrauding around slaughtering people left, right and centre. Your task is to travel around the three main areas of the camp – woods, lake and cave – in search of handy tools and weapons with which to defend yourself against this maniac. The game ends if Jason gets to the kids. Otherwise you can keep fighting as long as at least one counsellor remains alive.

## WEAPONS

Initially, counsellors are armed with **stones**, but other weapons to be found are a **knife**, a **machete**, an **axe**, a **torch** – Jason doesn't like light – and **pitchfork**.

## SPECIALS

Other items are a **flashlight** (handy in the cave), a **key**, a **lighter**, **vitamins** (that help heal wounds), a **sweater** (wear it and Jason won't harm you as it is his mother's) and **messages**.

## THE ENEMY

The *axeman* is not the only one you have to worry about. *Blood-sucking bats*, *callous crows*, *wolves* and *zombies* are definite health hazards. Jason's *long-dead mother* also wanders around.

## HINTS

1 Check out the interiors of the cabins carefully. Counsellors will move around by themselves during the game. You can switch between them, restore energy levels, and give them weapons.
2 Search large cabins for clues and weapons.
3 Start fires where possible. Jason is scared of them.
4 Keep track of where you are in the woods. It is easy to get lost.
5 Find the rowing boat to reach the isolated cabins at Lake Crystal.
6 Jason's supply of weapons can be found in the cave, but beware of Jason's mother.

## REMARKS

Not a brilliant tie-in from the hack 'n' slash movie. Gore hounds will be disappointed if they expect the film's red raw action.

## COMMENTS

PAUL: Totally tasteless, but when did lack of taste stop people playing games.
NIGEL: Never stopped me!
THAT'S NICE: Some interesting effects.
THAT'S A SHAME: Lacks addictive game play.

## GAUNTLET™

      7        4       7–70    1–2

## REVIEW

This is the Nintendo version of the arcade classic. The game that caused such a stir in the arcades a few years ago has transferred well to Nintendo, and it has all of the original features, with the obvious – and unavoidable – reduction in players.

## WEAPONS

There are four characters to choose from at the start, each with their own strengths and weaknesses. Wizard has **good magic** and **missiles**, but is a poor fighter – slow. Elf has **fair magic**, **good missiles**, and is a fair fighter – fast. Warrior has **poor magic**, **good missiles**, and is a good fighter – slow. Valkyrie is fair in everything.

Along the way these abilities can be enhanced by picking up the following: **armour**, which gives increased protection from attacks; **fight power**, bringing with it increased fighting ability; **magic** to cast a devastating spell; and **shot power** to increase missile attack.

## SPECIALS

**Invisibility** makes it harder for the bad guys to hit you. **Invulnerability** protects you from attack. **Reflective shots** bounce your arrows around the maze – very useful! **Repulsion** causes all the monsters to run away from you. **Super shots** – arrows kill everything in their path. **Stun traps**, the glowing floor sections temporarily paralyze you. **Traps**, the flashing floors will remove some walls if you stand on them.

## THE ENEMY

Loads of these in great variety. Watch out for the little black chap – he's not called *Death* for nothing!

## HINTS

1  Lots of the monsters need multiple hits to kill them . . . keep at it!
2  Shoot the little huts from which the monsters appear as soon as you can!
3  Some walls can be removed by shooting them.
4  If stumped, stand still for 10 seconds and all of the locked doors will open.
5  For a real cheat, try entering the code 42C BBI HZZ when playing the Warrior. This will take you straight to room 79, deep in the game.

## REMARKS

An all-time classic that has transferred well to the Nintendo. Particularly fun with two players.

## COMMENTS

JON: One of my all-time favourites.

# GOLGO 13™

8      2     7–70    1

## REVIEW

A Shoot'em Up/Beat'em Up with you playing the part of a famous secret agent. This game is apparently based on a Japanese comic book series, and the action is mainly horizontal scrolling, though now and again the perspective changes to a gun-sight view. A large game with a heavy leavening of adventure.

## WEAPONS

You start the game with a **small pistol** and a limited amount of ammo. Have no fear, for along the way you can pick up **ammo** – caches of 400 bullets are hidden here and there – and **grenades** – picked up from dead soldiers, they can blow away walls as well as people.

## SPECIALS

Not that many really: **infrared binoculars** that are good for seeing laser beams; **drinks** that replenish lost energy; and **keys** that unlock doors . . .

## THE ENEMY

They are real people so hence the Bad Taste warning. They come in ground-based and airborne forms, but watch out for the snipers in particular.

## HINTS

1 In direst emergency you can trade life points for bullets. Use the Select button to do this, but be very careful and don't overdo it!
2 Shooting innocent passers-by can yield useful information!
3 Your first cache of bullets can be found at the Potsdam subway station.
4 Make sure that you have at least three grenades before you go into the Action Maze.
5 When facing both ground and airborne enemies, concentrate on the ones on the ground first.

**6** Use the Jump Kick wherever possible to save bullets.

## REMARKS

An interesting variation on a theme but certainly not suitable for younger children.

## COMMENTS

THAT'S A SHAME: Gratuitous violence.

### IKARI WARRIORS™

        8                 7–70    1–2

## REVIEW

One of the élite band of all-time classics available on Nintendo. The game scrolls from top to bottom, you control an élite commando and you kill everything!

## WEAPONS

You start with just a **machine-gun** and 50 **grenades**. During the game you can find **super-bullets** to do more damage, **super-grenades** and **knives** that are good for close fighting.

## SPECIALS

There are four: **bullets** – look for the pistol icon; **energy** – look for the petrol can; **grenades** – find them at the Grenade symbol; and the **'K'** **symbol** – kills everything on screen . . . one use only.

## THE ENEMY

Everything from enemy *foot soldiers* to *super-tanks* and *attack helicopters*. They are realistic people, so think before you buy for very young children.

## HINTS

**1** Practise throwing the grenades – you have to be pretty good at it to get anywhere.
**2** To continue the game press the A  B  B  A buttons before 'Game Over' appears on the screen. You unfortunately lose all the special weapons that you have collected.

**3** In two player mode try this: put both players into the same tank, then get both of them to press their 'A' buttons at the same time and BINGO . . . Two tanks!

**4** Similarly both players should press both the A and B buttons when they arrive at the Heli-Pad . . . BINGO . . . Two helicopters!

## REMARKS

Still a good game after all these years.

## COMMENTS

JON: Brilliant – my all-time favourite.

PAUL: And 2000 is his all-time high score!

### IKARI WARRIORS II: VICTORY ROAD™

8          2          7–70          1–2

## REVIEW

The boys are back! This time they go into the far future to battle against evil Zang Zip, the War Dog. The game is much more complex and prettier.

## WEAPONS

Like the original, you start with a **machine gun** and 50 **grenades**. However, the special weapons have changed a little: **bazooka** – one shot but extremely powerful; **land mines** – lay them in front of the enemy . . . BOOOOOOM; **sword** – a magic one that spits fire and is generally all round mega do-do; and **arrow** – more like a ballistic missile, powerful but strictly one shot.

## SPECIALS

More of these than in the original as well. **Armour** repels the bullets . . . (most of the time!); **bonus** adds points to your score; **life power** restores lost energy; **thunderer** clears the entire screen of baddies – only one use though; **time** transports you to the Bar Shop; **wings** – you can now fly; and the **bar shop** where you can buy bits and pieces, or steal them, the choice is yours.

## THE ENEMY

Much more variation than the first game and, since they do not look at all like real people, a perfectly safe one for the kids.

## HINTS

1 Like the original you can continue by using the sequence A  B  B  A before 'Game Over' appears on the screen. It does not work on the last level, though.
2 Get a Quick Fire joystick by any means possible!
3 Practise your grenade-throwing.
4 Be thorough. There are a fair number of hidden features that need to be found.

## REMARKS

A worthy, if very different follow-up.

## COMMENTS

JON: An OK game, but not as good as the original.

### IRONSWORD: WIZARDS AND WARRIORS II™

    7       5     4–16    1

## REVIEW

This follow-up to the hit original sees you once more pitted against the evil wizard Malkil. This time you are on a quest to get back all the bits of the Iron Sword (a particularly Right-On weapon). Malkil has blagged it and hidden it in the realm of elements (that's Wind, Water, Fire and Earth to you and me). What's more, he's broken it into bits!

   The game scrolls from left to right. There are lots of things to kill and think about. What more could you want!

## WEAPONS

You start with just a **sword**, so you need to start looking for the **axe**, **helmet** and more **swords**. These are scattered throughout the game.

## SPECIALS

**Chickens** and **beer** replace lost energy. **Keys** open locks. **Super-boots** are just the thing for climbing that last mountain. **Magic bubbles** replace lost magic power. **Coins** can be traded at **inns**, where you can buy useful things and play a silly sub-game a bit like pinball.

## THE ENEMY

Each area is themed. There are lots of fiery things in the land of Fire and lots of birds in the Windy part – get it? The real challenges are the guardians at the end of each level. A special spell will allow you to destroy them. If you do not find this, the game is virtually impossible.

## HINTS

1 An asp's tongue spell cast in an inn yields interesting results.
2 The Dragon's Tooth provides food.
3 The familiar spell turns the baddies into piles of gold!
4 The four special spells to defeat the guardians are Windbane, Blightwater, Firesmite and Earthscorth.
5 When you are fighting guardians, there is a little blue line in the right hand corner of the screen. The smaller this gets, the closer you are to killing a guardian.
6 Collect as much money and as many keys as you can.
7 Study the map as well as you can.

## REMARKS

A very detailed and enjoyable game, but perhaps a little too difficult.

### JOHN ELWAY'S QUARTERBACK™

|   |   |      |     |
|---|---|------|-----|
| 2 | 7 | 8–70 | 1–2 |

## REVIEW

A simulation of American Football. If you happen to like this sport then this is a very good game.

Graphics and presentation in general are nothing special, but as the action is mostly of the thinking type, this does not matter too much. If you do not know much about American Football, this program will be a bit daunting.

## WEAPONS

None really, but there are extensive lists of Offensive and Defensive plays to choose from. Pick one of the plans on offer to control the game.

## THE ENEMY

The computer-controlled teams are always tough, but given time their actions become predictable.

## HINTS

A list of hints and tips here could become extremely complex, as the game reproduces the sports subtleties very well. If you're really keen, borrow a book on the sport from your local library. There are flaws in some of the carts that allow you to do some rather strange things.

From the 'play select' screen, move the cursor to the 'normal play/reverse play' box and leave it there. In a few moments you will return to the main screen. Now press the down arrow and the 'B' button at the same time. Your team will be able to move at twice their normal speed!

## REMARKS

An apparently bland game that can become quite addictive. A must for fans of the sport.

## COMMENTS

PAUL: Nice game.
JON: Rugby rip-off!
NIGEL: Nice game.
THAT'S NICE: Good to see a decent sports sim on the Nintendo.
THAT'S A SHAME: Two players can't play against each other!

JORDAN VS BIRD: ONE ON ONE™

9     3     7–70     1–2

## REVIEW

This game is a simulation of basketball with a difference. Instead of teams there is only one player on each side. The action is a faithful representation of the game but it is arcade based. The player actually controls the movements of the on-screen characters with the joystick, and therefore the game may not appeal to hardened simulation freaks. Having said that, the game is still very attractive and good fun to play.

## THE ENEMY

The two basketball players mentioned in the title are pretty good. Each of them has his own specialities that will leave anyone who has played the real thing gasping!

## HINTS

Try playing the game with the fouls removed until you have got used to the controls.

## REMARKS

A game that falls uncomfortably between Arcade and Simulation but is still a 'good laugh'.

KARNOV™

9    3    7–70    1

## REVIEW

Karnov is a circus strong man with the ability to produce fire balls from his mouth whenever he feels like it. As usual, Karnov's village has been plundered by a dragon and the 'Treasure of Babylon' stolen. Needless to say, Karnov is a bit miffed and sets off in hot pursuit through 9 horizontally scrolling levels in search of the dastardly fiend. The way the game looks is like the standard Beat'em Up model, but Karnov's fire balls are the main weapons. The graphics are nice. Like most games of this type, levels become progressively more difficult and Karnov is provided with an increasingly varied number of enemies to deal with, until he at last comes face to face with the Dragon in the final screen. Karnov starts the game with 3 lives, but fortunately the game comes with an unlimited number of continue options which you are going to need.

## WEAPONS

**Fire balls**, Karnov's standard weapon, are available in unlimited numbers right from the start. Karnov also has the services of no less than 10 special weapons/powers that he can utilize. These are found throughout the game. Most are one-shot and some are only available in certain areas. However, to make life a little easier, several can be stockpiled for later use, although only one may be used at a time. The specials available to you at any one time are premanently displayed on the screen, they are: a **ladder** to climb over things; **wings** to fly; **magic boots** to jump high; a **shield** that protects from attack; **bombs** to blow the baddies away; **boomerangs** that are viciously effective; and **Thunderclapper**, the mega weapon.

## SPECIALS

As well as the items mentioned above, there are also a number of power-ups scattered around the screens. These take the form of the letter 'K', (for Karnov!). Collect 50, and you get an extra life.

## THE ENEMY

The usual vast multitude!

## HINTS

1 Don't worry about not having the face mask when you go under water. It will only slow you down if you don't have it.
2 Flying Dragons can only be killed by a carefully placed head shot.
3 Although holes are usually bad news, there are some that hold a large number of K power-ups. There is one on level 3; the rest you will have to find.
4 Some trees can be climbed.
5 Boomerangs are very good against dinosaurs.
6 Look carefully and you can find over a dozen bombs right at the beginning of level 4.

## REMARKS

An enjoyable if not particularly outstanding game.

# KID KOOL™

| 7 | 4 | 6–16 | 1–2 | |

## REVIEW

A Mario Bros. clone. The graphics are big and cute, and the violence is all heavily disguised. Despite the fact that this game is a blatant copy of the Bros., it remains a very enjoyable game, especially since unlimited continues are provided!

## WEAPONS

You start the game with **Wickie**. This is a small round creature that you usually carry under your arm. When danger threatens, simply take out Wickie and throw him at the baddies like a bowling ball. Silly, but very effective!

## SPECIALS

Absolutely herds of these, but you will have to find them for yourselves.

## THE ENEMY

All the usual cutesie rabble.

## HINTS

1 Hone your jumping skills to perfection – you're going to need them.
2 The beach houses make very good makers for judging jumps over water. When you reach the beach house, jump.
3 Believe it or not, the Kid can run on water, (sometimes)!
4 Search through the grass at the beginning of each level, you may find a bonus Wickie.

## REMARKS

Blatantly derivative but great fun. Well worth buying if you've already done the Bros. duo.

7      3      6–16      1–2

## REVIEW

Another obscure Cutesie arcade game converted for the Nintendo. The plot line is almost incomprehensible, but seems to revolve around the rescue of the Princess. She has been kidnapped by the evil wizard, who has hidden her at the end of 7 levels of vertical scrolling action. You start the game with 3 lives and a 6-minute time limit in which to complete each level.

## WEAPONS

Your basic weapon is a **sword** which is perfectly adequate against most enemies, if a little weedy against some of the nasty guardians at the end of each level.

## SPECIALS

There are five of these: **coins** to add to your overall score; a **golden bell** that kills enemies at an increased range; the **Small Kid Niki** and **Small Princess** who bring extra life; a **silver bell** that kills all enemies on screen (usable only once); and a **scroll** that allows access to the next level.

## THE ENEMY

Each level has its own unique guardian as well as hordes of other nasties. A few of these are *Chubbies, Kites, Foxes, Coin Birds, Masked Birds, Devils, Ogi Birds*.

## HINTS

**1** The baddies and traps have been positioned to make it very difficult to get into any kind of rhythm with the controller. There *are* patterns, but they are very complex. Stop each time to access things before you leap!

**2** The Stone Witch on level 3 *can* be killed! Although she keeps breaking into small versions of herself, keep going – you will get there in the end!

**3** The Stone Wizard can only be killed when the fire is burning. Keep attacking until it goes out. Then wait for another fire and attack again. Keep doing this and he will eventually go.

**4** The Green Grub can be a bit of a problem. To kill him, knock off all his body segments, and then simply polish off the head.

**5** As usual, you don't have to kill everything – a lot of baddies can simply be avoided by jumping over them.

**6** Watch out for baddies sneaking up behind you, especially on the later levels.

## REMARKS

Just another cutesie game. Good fun to play but not as good as the Mario Bros.

## COMMENTS

JON: I really hate this game.

PAUL: That's only because he's rubbish at it!

### KNIGHT RIDER™

    7        4      7–70     1

## REVIEW

Does anyone remember the TV series 'Knight Rider'? It involved the adventures of Michael Knight and a super car, called KITT!

What we have here is a 'Race'em Up'. The player sees the action through the windscreen of the car and must not only drive the car very fast but also shoot, and preferably hit, all manner of bad guy vehicles along the way. Like most such games, there are numerous add on features for your vehicle to be obtained at the start of each level during a special kitting out session! There is a large choice, but space is limited.

There are a number of different missions to complete and at the start you are supplied with 3 lives. There is a limited amount of time in which to complete all the missions.

## WEAPONS

There are **machine-guns** with unlimited supplies of ammo. These are pretty feeble. The **missiles** have limited ammo, but they are very effective, especially against airborne targets. Then there is the **laser** – the ultimate weapon!

Your car has a top speed of 250 mph, and **turbo** is available for even faster sprints – only in a limited number. A **radar scanner** warns of enemies approaching up to 10 miles in any direction.

## SPECIALS

From time to time a **black lorry** will appear in front of you. It looks exactly the same as one of the enemy's except for a small Knight Rider logo, so be careful. By driving up behind it, it is possible to collect a number of power-up items. These take the form of letters that must be collected by being caught on your bonnet.

**I** Extra life.

**G** Fills up petrol tank.

**L** 20 additional laser bursts.

**M** 20 additional missiles.

**R** Repairs any damage sustained by KITT.

**T** Adds 30 seconds to the time allowed for this section.

## THE ENEMY

These all take the form of some kind of vehicle: *jeeps, helicopters, sports cars, cadillacs, planes, tankers, lorries.* There are also *Terminators* – large black lorries that are very tough. They serve the function of guardians at the end of each level. *Karrs* are the enemy equivalents of KITT.

As well as enemies you will encounter innocent bystanders. Shooting these will remove 5 seconds from your available time so is not to be encouraged. Bystanders take various forms, but will always have some blue in their colour scheme.

## HINTS

**1** Learn by your mistakes. Observe why you lost a level and then think about the special times you chose at the start.

**2** Use the turbo, but be careful. It uses up a lot of petrol!

**3** Look out for the Knight Foundation lorry. It is very easy to miss.

## REMARKS

A fairly standard Race'em Up game. Good fun if you like that sort of thing, but not outstanding.

7       4     6–16   1–2

## REVIEW

This game is a cross between a Beat 'em Up and a cutesie arcade adventure – Double Dragon meets the Mario Bros. perhaps? The story revolves around the rescue of a kidnapped princess and takes you through a total of 8 levels of action. As usual, there are 3 lives to start with and loads of bits and bobs to pick up along the way.

## WEAPONS

You start with just the ability to *punch* things. However, there are a vast number of add-on specials to be found along the way.

## SPECIALS

**E Bells** – collect 5 for an extra life. The **crystal ball** weakens Golems (snipers). **Beads** allow you to see the invisible coffins. The **candle** allows you to see traps. **Gun Ball** is a useful ranged weapon. The **mirror** shields you against some enemy attacks, while '**P**' and '**K**' adds power to your attacks. **POW** increases your energy level and '**?**' is the mystery bonus. **Sake** slows down the enemy Dragon. **Scroll A** used with the 'K' symbol allows you to kill the Ware Cat; **Scroll B** slows down the Inigon; while the **sword** kills the Dragon clan. The **treasure box** contains POW and occasionally extra weapons.

## THE ENEMY

Over 30 different varieties all with different abilities. These are just some: *Ware Cat* is really tough – use the Scroll A and 'K'. *Bison Commandos* are hard case heroes, so try using a 'K' power-up attack. *Gunman* is fairly weak, but watch out for that gun! *Thunder Bolts* – RUN AWAY!!! *Mr Coffin* is persistent, but should not cause too much trouble.

## HINTS

**1** To use the sword, press both buttons and then the arrow key in the direction you wish to attack.

**2** To continue the game, wait for the title screen. Then press the 'A' button and 'Start' together.

**3** Directions of kick can be changed in mid air.

**4** Do not progress to the higher levels until you have collected enough power. A level of 3 is recommended.

## REMARKS

An absorbing and very addictive game that is well worth a look.

## COMMENTS

NIGEL: Great game!

THAT'S NICE: Loads of different monsters!!

LEE TREVINO'S FIGHTING GOLF™

8     5     8–70     1–4

## REVIEW

LTFG is a golf game and a pretty good one at that. You have the choice of playing with up to four contestants while the other players are controlled by the computer. You also have a choice of two full 18-hole courses and all the usual strokes and clubs. Only the 2 iron and 3 wood are missing which does not detract in any way from the games playability or realism. The scoring system can be either the standard 'Par' rating or the 'Nassau' system.

## WEAPONS

To strike the ball, three presses of the fire button are required to set the club swinging, to hit the ball and to follow through. By varying the timing of these it is possible to fully control where the ball will go.

    The choice of the club will obviously vary the distance the ball will travel. In general, **woods** hit the ball long and low while **irons** hit it shorter and higher. The higher the club's number the less distance it will travel. **Wedges** travel the shortest and highest, and **putters** are only really useful on the greens.

## SPECIALS

There are all the usual hazards of golf. The **rough** is just that and will reduce the distance you can hit the ball, so it is best to try an iron rather than a wood. **Bunkers** are worse, the wedge being about the best club to use. Hitting the **water** costs you a penalty – the ball is put back where it started, and a stroke is added to your score.

## HINTS

**1** Learn to control the ball properly. Soon you will be able to use Hook and Slice to your own advantage.
**2** Study the wind direction before hitting the ball.
**3** Learn which clubs are best at which job.
**4** The clubs recommended only work if the shot is hit perfectly. If in doubt, reselect.
**5** If you need a perfect hit to avoid a particular hazard, try playing safe and hitting the ball short.
**6** Experiment with the four different players provided, they each have strengths and weaknesses.

## REMARKS

A nice game if you like golf!

## COMMENTS

NIGEL: I like golf and I like this game.

LEGACY OF THE WIZARD™

6      4      6–16      1

## REVIEW

A cutesie game with a fantasy theme. The game takes you through a total of 4 levels or 'Worlds' with the normal 3 lives.

## WEAPONS

As is often the case, all you have is your fists.

## SPECIALS

Loads!! . . . These are just some. **Bread** replenishes lost energy. A **cross** kills all the enemies on screen. You need the **potion** to cast spells, while a **ring** gives you temporary invincibility. **Keys** open locked doors and chests.

As well as the more mundane specials, there are also a number of one-offs. These can be found just lying around but are more often in locked chests. **Armour** provides extra protection, and you can actually just walk through some weaker monsters. The **elixir** completely restores your energy levels. The **magic bottle** completely restores your magic level. The **shield** deflects all monster attacks. Collect 4 **crowns** to receive a Dragon Slayer, and a **Dragon Slayer** kills Dragons! The **power knuckle** increases your attack power, and **gloves** allow you to move blocks around and therefore solve the mazes.

## THE ENEMY

As well as the fairly ordinary ones there are 4 end-of-level guardians: *Archwinger*, a flying lizard; *Erebone*, a ghost; *Rockgaea*, king of the rocks; and *Tarantunes*, a huge demon spider.

## HINTS

A nice touch in this game is the ability to call on other members of your family to help you out during the game. Their abilities are as follows: **Xemm** (Father), a good warrior who can use the gloves. **Meyna** (Mother), who is a powerful magic user and able to fly! **Roas** (Son), a great warrier, who can use the Dragon Slayer. **Lyll** (Daughter), a lesser magic user. **Pochi** (Pet Master), who apparently thinks he is a dog! **Grandmother**, who knows the save game password. **Grandfather** – tell him the password to save the game.

If you get stuck but want to see what it is like deep in the game try using this password: GZLL LDLW MKYI HQRD POHJ IEIM ESCY TKGA.

## REMARKS

A lovely cutesie adventure game with a few novel twists. Definitely recommended for younger players.

## COMMENTS

JON: Just about my level this – great!
THAT'S NICE: Having all the family around to help out.

8    2    6–16    1–2

## REVIEW

A Shoot 'em Up that looks like a Beat 'em Up, and very much in the mould of the arcade classic, 'R Type'. Play scrolls alternately horizontally and vertically which is good. There are the usual 3 lives and the option to have 2 players playing at the same time, although this strains the Nintendo's abilities to the limit graphically.

## WEAPONS

There are two to start off with: a **gun** for rapid fire, but it is a bit weedy; and a **cannon**, which is slow to fire but very powerful. Only the gun may be used in the horizontal sections.

## SPECIALS

All the usual power-ups are available.

## THE ENEMY

Fantasy-type stuff.

## HINTS

1 Don't shoot the statues; they turn into nasty flying things!
2 Watch out for the 'continue' power-ups, you are going to need them.
3 Try walking into some of the whirlwinds. Interesting things can happen!
4 If you reach the bonus stage, speed is of the essence, or you will become trapped.

## REMARKS

An OK game if you like this sort of thing. There were a lot of gremlins in the game we played, with the collision detection programming seeming to be particularly suss. The instruction manual is also a mess.

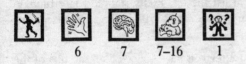

## REVIEW

This classic has maintained its position as a front-runner in the Nintendo game catalogue for some time. Graphically poor, its strengths are in plot and the excellent balance of reflex and brain work. It also benefits from having a 'save game' option.

## WEAPONS

Too many to go into great detail, but they include the following: **three swords** – a normal all-purpose skewer, a white sword with twice-hitting power and a magic blue sword that has four times the power of the basic blade. **A letter to a little old lady**! – give her this in the cave. A **bomb**: booom! A **boomerang** to chuck at the enemy. The **bow & arrows** – for each arrow shot, Link loses a ruby. You definitely need this weapon, some enemies can only be beaten by it. The **magic wand** casts some useful spells. Keep 'em peeled for the **magic book**. The **power bracelet** can help you lift rocks etc.

## SPECIALS

Loads and loads! **Candles** – blue ones light one screen, red candles will last longer. Try tossing a few against the bad guys. The **compass** points out the direction of the Triforce. **Enemy bait** works against most of the enemy. A **heart** will give you a free life. **Keys** open doors; the magic one (with the lion's head) is re-useable time and time again. The **ladder** can be used to get across holes or a river. The **magic lock** stops the enemy from entering the screen you are in. Use a **map** to find out where you are. The **raft** is great for rivers and lakes, and must be launched from a dock. **Rings** – red ones reduce Link's damage by a quarter and blue ones by a half. Grab as many **rubies** as you can – the blue ones are worth five times the yellow. You can't have more than 255 at a time. **Water of Life** turns white hearts back to red. The **whistle** can open things up or scare things away! It summons the whirlwind after you have found the last piece of the Triforce.

## THE ENEMY

So many it is impossible to list the lot. Pretty standard fare though. One clue only – kill the *Chief Ghost* and his underlings will disappear!

## HINTS

**1** There is a second quest after you have collected all the bits of the Triforce. It uses many of the same screens, but there are more enemies! If you want in, straight away, type 'ZELDA' when you register at the start.

**2** Even though it's a one-player game, keep the second controller plugged in, as there are a few surprises in store. First, cancel any game by entering into the sub-screen and pressing Controller 2's button *and* the Control Pad at the same time; second, and this is a bit trickier, when you meet the old man in the cave and he asks you to pay, go to the sub-screen and push buttons A and B together on Controller 2. You'll get out without paying!

**3** Try to fight at a distance, or you will lose life points too quickly. Sneaking up from behind is a good idea. Remember, if the enemy can't touch you, they can't hurt you.

**4** The blue ring must be bought in a secret room under Armos.

**5** You will need to enter the waterfall to find out where the white sword is hidden.

**6** If you drop bombs close enough to the Dodongos they will eat them and explode! If you are too scared to get that close, then use the bombs to stun them and then go in with the sword. Use bombs on Manhandia but make sure you hit it in the centre.

**7** Gleeok can only be hurt by attacking its necks or heads.

**8** OK, here's the one you really wanted! The sword is hidden under a gravestone in the cemetery.

## REMARKS

Useful to have unlimited Continues during normal play. Good music, and great sound effects too!

## COMMENTS

JON: Getting a bit long in the tooth?
PAUL: Look who's talking!

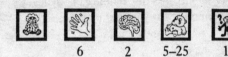

| 6 | 2 | 5–25 | 1 |

## REVIEW

A typical cutesie adventure based around the escapades of Mappy the policeman. Apparently, thieves have stolen the engagement ring that he has bought for his girlfriend, Mapico. Mappy sets out to retrieve the ring.

The ensuing game sees you trying to achieve this goal. The whole thing is delightfully silly and sports some very nice graphics indeed. To help the younger players there is an extensive demo mode to take you right through the game and tell you how to restart if you get stuck. There is also a limitless continue option that should come in handy.

## WEAPONS

Lots of silly ones! **Toys, pish, gold coins** . . . etc, etc!!!

## SPECIALS

**Fireworks** blow everything on the screen away. Use **pullies** to swing from screen to screen. **Fishes** hypnotize the cats! **Torches** get rid of ghosts. Finally, **bowling balls**: can be thrown at the enemy.

## THE ENEMY

The two main baddies are *Nyamco* and *Murky*. Murky always appears as a cat. Nyamco on the other hand adopts a number of disguises: Railroad Town Station Master; Wild West Cowboy; Tropical World Big Chief; Jungle Wild Boy; Pirate World Pirate; Ghost Town Mummy or Vampire; Seventh Avenue Waiter and Milky Town Guardsman.

## HINTS

1 Be careful to search all areas. You may find yourself stuck later on because you have missed something.
2 Monsters always follow the same patterns. Learning these will make life a lot easier.
3 You can move from floor to floor, using the special trampolines, but you will only be able to bounce three times before losing a life.

## REMARKS

A great cutesie game very much in the mould of 'Mickey's Mousecapade'. Strongly recommended for younger players.

## COMMENTS

THAT'S NICE: Great cutesie graphics.

THAT'S A SHAME: Instruction manual a bit naff.

### MARBLE MADNESS

| | | | | |
|---|---|---|---|---|
| 9 | 4 | 6–60 | 1–2 | |

## REVIEW

The Nintendo version of the classic arcade game. Just in case you haven't heard of it (where have you been for the last few years!), the game entails guiding a marble through a maze of slopes within a set time period. It all sounds very easy until you actually try doing it!

The graphics are particularly nice, but be warned – this game is difficult!

## SPECIALS

**Wands** – these appear randomly and will give a 10-second bonus to your time.

## THE ENEMY

Apart from the actual maze itself, which is hard enough, there are also a number of other hazards: *Marble Munchers* look like coiled springs but they will attempt to eat you. *Black Marbles* try to get in your way and slow you down; either avoid them or push them over an edge to get a time bonus.

## HINTS

1 Get very clever with the controller! Timing is everything.
2 Time bonuses are cumulative. To succeed in the higher levels you will need a fair amount of time accumulated from the lower levels.
3 If you really get stuck, put the game into 2-player mode. This way you will always win the game and receive the end-time bonus.

## REMARKS

An excruciatingly hard game but immensely addictive.

# COMMENTS

PAUL: Great game but just too hard.

JON: Agreed!

NIGEL: Not 'arf!!

THAT'S A SHAME: Game just too hard – or are we just a bunch of wimps?

## MEGA MAN 2™

8      4      8–60      1

## REVIEW

A universally praised game, Mega Man 2 is a sprawling Arcade Adventure very much in the mould of the Mario Bros. series (see Review). The game is platform-based with a horizontally scrolling screen. As a bonus, there are lots of things to pick up along the way and you have the ability to shoot things as well. You start the game with 3 lives.

The plot revolves around Mega's battle against the Evil Doctor Willy. This time, the fiend has protected himself with 9 worlds, each guarded by a super robot with a special power. Mega must complete all 9 worlds and their guardians before the final show-down with Willy himself. As each guardian is destroyed Mega may collect a special power that will help him in the rest of the game.

At the end of each level, a password is provided that will allow you to restart the game at the same point that you left it. Mega is provided with an energy level that reduces when he is hit. If it is reduced to zero he is dead.

## WEAPONS

Mega Man has a fairly weedy **gun** that he can use from the start. Other weapons must be picked up along the way. All weapons have a limited energy supply that may be replenished along the way (see Specials).

## SPECIALS

**Air Shooter** (from Air Man World) is a gun that shoots out tornadoes.
**Bubble Lead** (from Bubble Man World) throws a bubble that then

73

rolls along the screen in front of you. Destroys most things! **Atomic Fire** (from Heat Man World) is a fire ball gun. Pressing Fire for longer increases the power. **Crash Bomber** (from Crash Man World) has bombs that can be thrown at walls. Blasts a hole through some but not all. Get out of the way before they detonate! **Metal Blade** (from Metal Man World) throws saw blades at the enemy! **Leaf Shield** (from Wood Man World) surrounds you with a shield made of leaves. **Boomerang** (from Quick Man World) is lethal when thrown at the enemy. **Time Stopper** (from Flash Man World) temporarily freezes all the enemy on screen.

These specials are all collected from the relevant end-of-level guardians. In addition, the following may be found scattered about throughout the game: **energy pellets, crystals, balls** that refresh Mega's energy level when he walks over them. **Energy crystals** that recharge energy as above but may be kept and used when required. **1-Up** is a mini version of Mega himself. Run over him for an extra life. The **elevator**, when placed against a wall, will go up . . . and up – a very useful way to progress through some of the levels. The **Jet Sled** which you set from Air Man means that you will be able to fly over hazards later in the game. The **Levitation Platform** can be acquired, one from Heat Man.

## THE ENEMY

There are many. The main enemy on each level is covered in Specials, and are of course the hardest!

## HINTS

1 Start with Air Man or Bubble Man, as they seem to be a little easier.
2 Get the Air Sled before attempting Heat Man.
3 Do not jump over Lantern Fish, walk through them.
4 Use your power-up times wisely.
5 In Wood World, the first Atomic Chickens can be avoided simply by standing close to the ledges. If you do that, they do not seem to notice you and will jump straight over your head.
6 Since the worlds do not have to be completed in any particular order, don't get disheartened if you get stuck. Try playing a different world, as there may be a special time there to help you.
7 Right from the start, try using the passwords A1 C4 D1 D3 D5 E1 E2 E3 E4 for super powers. The password system in Mega

74

Man uses a grid. Rows are referred to using the letters and columns using numbers.

## METAL GEAR™

7        5        7–70        1

## REVIEW

This is a Shoot 'em Up very much in the style of 'Ikari Warriors'. The plot follows the escapades of one Solid Snake who, the story tells us, is an ex-Marine on a mission to destroy an evil super weapon. This weapon is hidden deep in a multi-level fortress guarded by the usual herds of nasties.

The game comes with the usual 3 lives for the player and a whole host of add-on weapons and an adequate presentation. Since the game is hard, it is provided with a limitless Continue option.

## WEAPONS

Loads, but the game is so difficult we never managed to get any!

## SPECIALS

Look out for the **pass cards** dotted about the screen. These allow you access to some of the restricted buildings.

## THE ENEMY

All the usual fodder. *Infantry* in several varieties, *tanks* etc.

## HINTS

1 Be sure to rescue all the hostages you can. Killing them reduces your ability to carry ammunition, which can be fatal later in the game.
2 To beat tanks, try running out in front of them, dropping a mine, and then running away again. It is not foolproof, however!
3 Watch out for the security cameras at later levels – they shoot lasers at you!

## REMARKS

Ordinary game with an irritatingly large number of typing errors in the instructions. OK, but not a patch on the very similar 'Ikari Warriors'.

6　　　2　　　5–20　　　1

## REVIEW

This is a game designed for young children based on Mickey and Minnie Mouse. It is a platform-based Arcade Adventure game with minimal violence and cutesie characters. In a nutshell, Minnie has been kidnapped and you must rescue her. You start off with 5 lives and may begin the game at the start of any of the 5 levels.

## WEAPONS

None – officially that is. In fact, you throw nice shiny little stars at the enemy. You have to pick these up along the way.

## SPECIALS

**Extra lives** that are invisible to start with, appear when hit by a star. **Cake** increases your energy level. A **diamond** destroys all enemies when thrown. The invisible **Guardian Angel** will give you 10 seconds of invulnerability, and **keys** unlock doors.

## THE ENEMY

Loads of the usual cutesie fodder. They look sweet but can be very dangerous. Beware especially the waves in the sea section!

## HINTS

1 Look for Lamps as they often contain either Cakes or Diamonds.
2 Practise your jumping, as monsters can be avoided this way.
3 Not every baddie can be destroyed – try jumping over them.
4 To start the game at the level of your choice, press Select and a direction key at the same time during the title screen. Depending on the direction selected, you will go to the following:
Up, Select & Start – Castle.
Right, Select & Start – Ocean.
Down, Select & Start – Ship.
Left, Select & Start – Woods.

# MILON'S SECRET CASTLE™

   7        5       6–16      1

## REVIEW

This game is all about mazes. Each level has two of them, and they contain all manner of interesting things. There are 7 levels in all, and a number of shops in which to purchase add-ons.

## WEAPONS

A nondescript forward-firing **pop-gun** is all you have to start with. However, once into the game you will have the chance to increase its power by killing one of the chief demons.

## SPECIALS

There are two kinds in this game, the ones you find and the ones you buy. The finders are: **coins** to be used to buy things from the shop; a **honeycomb** that increases your energy; **crystal balls** that increase your shot power (you need to collect 7 of them to win the game); the **bee** provides an invulnerable shield for a limited period; the umbrella fires rapid shots.

The ones you buy include: a **fireproof vest**, a **lantern**, **paint**, a **canteen** and a **balloon**.

## THE ENEMY

The *demons* are the hardest of the lot. The rest are the usual fantasy characters with a hint of cutesie thrown in for good measure.

## HINTS

1 Demons are difficult to shoot down. Keep at it – you will get there in the end.
2 When in a maze, shoot at everything.

## REMARKS

This is one of those games that does not look anything special, but is in fact immensely addictive. If you like a challenge, then this one is for you. If you tend to be impatient with puzzles, avoid it at all costs!

## COMMENTS

## NFL FOOTBALL™

| 5 | 8 | 10–70 | 1 |

### REVIEW

An American Football game with the emphasis very much on strategy rather than joystick bashing. With no less than 20 offensive plays and 16 defensive plays this game really does offer a lot of possibilities.

### THE ENEMY

The computer-controlled team is very good, so unless you are very lucky, it will be a fair few games before you manage to beat it.

### HINTS

Do use the practice field to hone your skills and try to keep your game balanced evenly between passing and running.

### REMARKS

Excellent in-depth sports simulation. Get yourself a book on American Football tactics and go the whole hog!

## 1943: THE BATTLE OF MIDWAY™

| 8 | 2 | 7–70 | |

### REVIEW

The game's title comes from the World War II Battle of the Midway and you control a fighter bomber called a *Lightning* and must single-handedly destroy hordes of enemy planes and ships. Surprisingly for a game originally designed in Japan, it casts the hero as American and the baddies as Japanese!

The game is seen from above with the screen scrolling from top to bottom. Players start with 3 lives, each with an independent energy level. Energy levels can be built up by numerous power-ups that are scattered along the way. All in all, there are 23 levels of action each with its own end-of-level super-meanie. At the start of the game, players are given a limited opportunity to customize their plane. It is possible to allot up to 3 extra energy points to a particular feature of the plane:

*Offensive Power* increases the power of the basic weapon.
*Defensive Power* increases the *Lightening*'s ability to absorb damage.
*Energy Level* increases your overall energy level.
*Special Weapons* increases the power of special weapons.
*Time Limit* extends the life of temporary special weapons.

## WEAPONS

At the start of the game you are equipped with a basic but effective forward-firing machine-gun. There are numerous chances to pick up special weapons during the game. The weapons are acquired simply by flying over the relevant symbol as it appears on screen (for details of how to find the symbols, see the Specials section). **Auto** has the same effect as using an auto-fire joystick. **Shotgun** destroys enemy bullets as well as the actual enemy. **Super shell** is a large cannon that is particularly effective against ships and larger aircraft. **Scatter cannon** shoots in 3 directions at the same time.

Special Weapons are of limited duration, though this time may be extended by allotting energy points to the Time Limit part of the opening section. If you collect a special weapon symbol whilst already using a special weapon, the *Lightning* will discard the old one and start using the new weapon immediately.

## SPECIALS

The basic special appears first on the screen as a small symbol marked 'POW'. Flying over this will restore lost energy. However, if you shoot the symbol it will change to any one of several others that represent different special features. A symbol can be changed as much as you like by shooting it until you find the one you want.

The POW symbols appear in one of two ways. Either they simply appear, or they are awarded when a whole wave of fighters is destroyed. Specials available are: **Energy Tank** that restores extra lost energy; the **Side Fighter** which adds an extra *Lightning* at your side (known as Wingman); and **Super Pow** which restores your energy level to full.

Like the special weapons mentioned above, the Wingman is only temporary. As well as these 'normal' specials, there are also a small number of bizarre specials floating round: **spacemen, barrel, cat, cow, flower, star, strawberry**. Simply fly over them to collect a bonus.

## THE ENEMY

Baddies come in a wide variety of shapes and sizes but fall into the following categories:

*Small planes* appear in predictable patterns and in swarms. One shot to kill. Red ones are the most dangerous.

*Bombers* appear singly or in pairs. Multi hits to kill. All can fire back as well as forward. The bigger they are, the more dangerous and difficult they are to kill.

*Ships* all have a number of turrets that shoot at you. All turrets must be destroyed to destroy the ship.

End-of-level baddies are a law unto themselves. Please refer to the Hints section.

## HINTS

**1** Pressing both of the fire buttons at once causes the *Lightning* to 'loop'. This is very useful for manœuvering out of a tight spot.

**2** Use the *Lightning* bomb sparingly. It is very useful for softening up some of the tougher end-of-level meanies.

**3** The best position on the screen to place the *Lightning* is about two-thirds of the way down. In early levels you can stay right at the bottom, but later on planes come at you from the bottom as well as the top, so watch out!

**4** Some of the big bombers need to be shot in the engines to destroy them. Flames appear when the engine has been hit. Be warned though, some of them need to have up to 50 shots in the body as well!

**5** Try shooting the clouds as there are POW symbols hidden behind some of them.

**6** Use an auto-fire joystick!

**7** Use the password TY19U to go straight to the final level.

## REMARKS

A very good version of the arcade game. Brilliant if Shoot 'em Ups are your thing; well worth a look even if they are not. Be warned, this game is very addictive.

## COMMENTS

JON: Another one of my all-time favourites.

THAT'S A SHAME: No two player option.

### OPERATION WOLF™

| 8 | 2 | 7–70 | | | 1 | |

## REVIEW

With such a well-known game, it almost seems redundant to describe it, but for those of you out there who've been in Albania for the last three years here it is.

You play the part of the usual American superhero who, armed with only his trusty machine-gun and a handful of grenades, must single-handedly rescue 6 hostages from the evil clutches of Latin American terrorists.

The view of the game is that of the superhero and he never appears on screen during the actual game. The screen scrolls slowly from left to right with the enemy appearing just about everywhere. There are 4 levels in all, each with 6 separate sections. The sections are repeated, but with an increase in the numbers of the enemy after completion. The sections take you through the following settings: Communications Centre, Jungle, Village, Ammo Dump, Prison Camp and Airport.

There are no end-of-level guardians, and each screen is completed when the opposition has been wiped out. As well as the usual score display there is a useful count kept of how many enemy remain to be destroyed before a particular section is completed. There is also a yellow line stretching along the bottom of the screen that turns an ominous red as you collect wounds. If it turns completely red, you are dead! To complete an entire level it is not necessary to rescue any hostages at all. All you have to do is complete all 6 sections and remain alive. However, your score will be very low unless some hostages are rescued.

81

## WEAPONS

At the start our hero is armed only with a **machine-gun** and a handful of **grenades**. Ammunition and spare grenades may be collected by shooting the various items as they appear throughout the game. A magazine contains 20 shots and a grenade is just that – a grenade. There is a screen display that informs you how many magazines and grenades you have at any one time.

## SPECIALS

Throughout the game a number of special features appear. Like ammunition, they are activated simply by shooting them; though be warned, with some of them it requires more than one hit to activate them. A **bottle** reduces the number of wounds. **Dynamite** kills all enemy on the screen. 'Free' is a mega machine-gun that blasts for 10 seconds. It does not use up ammunition and fires at twice the normal rate. **Pigs, chickens** and **vultures**, if shot repeatedly will drop ammunition that may then be collected in the normal manner.

## THE ENEMY

These take all kinds of form, from the lowly **foot soldier** to a **helicopter**. Most foot soldiers only require one, or at most two, hits to kill them. Helicopters require many more. From time to time civilians will appear on screen. These take various guises (nurses, small children etc.) and should not be shot at. Hitting one of these will give you extra wounds. Now and again, an enemy general will appear using a civilian as a shield, so be careful.

## HINTS

1 Some soldiers throw knives and grenades at you; shoot them before they hit and no damage is received.
2 Try to use grenades only on larger enemy targets. It is particularly satisfying to throw one in among several tanks!
3 When rescuing prisoners (Section 5) always kill the soldier that is carrying a knife; if you don't he will kill the hostage.
4 Now and again, an armoured soldier appears wearing a flak jacket and wielding a very large machine-gun. He can only be killed by shooting him in the head or by using a grenade.
5 Try to shoot parachutists before they land; they are a lot easier to hit and they don't usually shoot back.

## REMARKS

The Light Zapper makes the game much more playable and helps to keep the feel of the arcade original. Although the game can be played with the standard controller which projects a target cross-hair onto the screen, it is not as much fun.

## COMMENTS

NIGEL: A brilliant game in its original arcade version, Operation Wolf on the Nintendo is a fair game in its own right. With the Light Zapper it is very good. Buy it!

JON: I love this game and can't wait for the variants to come out!

PAUL: And I thought you guys were peace-loving softies.

THAT'S NICE: Light Zapper add-on.

THAT'S A SHAME: Graphics not so hot.

### PAC MAN™

| 8 | 5 | 7–70 | 1–2 |

## REVIEW

A faithful copy of the old arcade classic, Pac Man has you in control of the odd pie-shaped creature as he rushes around the mazes. Hotly pursued by a number of Ghosts, Pac Man's main objective is to survive. Around the maze are a number of dots and special items. The dots score points when collected and all the dots must be collected in order to progress to the next level. Pac Man collects things by simply moving over them.

## WEAPONS

None. Pac Man attacks things by moving over them. However he can only attack ghosts when they are blue.

## SPECIALS

Scattered around the screen are a number of **magic pills**. When Pac Man moves over these all of the Ghosts on screen temporarily turn blue. As long as they remain this colour, he can attack them and score points into the bargain. Should he touch them at any other time, he is destroyed. As well as the pills, **bunches of fruit** also appear, these have no special effect but do score points if eaten.

## THE ENEMY

The *Ghosts* are the only enemies in this game. They wander around the screen in a seemingly random manner, until you get too close. They will then lock on and follow. At first they move a lot slower than you, but as you progress from level to level, the difference in speed decreases.

## HINTS

**1** Study how the Ghosts move and you will begin to see patterns. These can be exploited to win the game.
**2** Save the magic pills until there are a number of Ghosts nearby.
**3** Try to keep as far away from the Ghosts as possible!

## REMARKS

A faithful, if somewhat limited, copy of the arcade original. But there are only 6 levels and the game is nearly impossible at the higher levels, so unless you are a real fan, give this one a miss.

PHANTOM FIGHTER™

8      2      7–17      1

## REVIEW

This is a standard Kung Fu Beat 'em Up. The presentation is very attractive, with particularly nice graphics. For a change the enemy are ghosts! There are 8 different levels, with a big, bad guardian at the end of each.

## WEAPONS

The normal **punch** and **kick** to start with. As you progress through the game a number of **scrolls** will be discovered. These can be traded in for lessons at the 'Martial Arts Academy'. Here you can be trained to have stronger punches and kicks. The **Sacred Sword** is very useful, but only useable for a limited period.

## SPECIALS ·

Very few of these by modern standards! The **talisman** is a single-use guardian freezer! The **mirror** temporarily paralyzes the enemy. You need to collect three **jades** before you can enter the guardian's house.

## THE ENEMY

*Kyonshies*, or Japanese ghosts, are the enemy in this game. There are over a dozen different ones, each with their own strengths and weaknesses. Watch out for the baby ghosts. You can kill them, but they can also be befriended!

## HINTS

**1** Patterns are very difficult to work out – think before you leap!
**2** Try not to stand and fight if you do not have to. Movement is the name of the game!

## REMARKS

A very ordinary Beat 'em Up, lifted by the amusing antics of the enemy and excellent graphics.

PLATOON™

8    4    9–90    1

## REVIEW

The game of the film and, for once, the game is as good as the film. The game is a blend of uncompromising Shoot 'em Up action and strong mystery. There are 4 levels to progress through, and you score points for finding things as well as shooting them! The number of lives varies from level to level.

## WEAPONS

As the game attempts to be realistic there is not much room for mega add-ons. The ones there are tend to be rather mundane in appearance and are concerned with solving particular puzzles.

## SPECIALS

**Ammo** restores used ammunition. **First Aid** repairs damage or your platoon members. **Explosives** blow up the bridge, and the **torch** and **map** are essential for exploring the tunnels. As well as being useful in themselves, simply finding these things scores points.

## THE ENEMY

Real people! *Viet Cong guerillas* and *NVA soldiers*. There are a fair number of innocent bystanders, so be careful. This is real killing and carries a very strong bad taste warning. Not on for young children.

## HINTS

1 Look before you shoot. Kill 6 civilians and the game is over.
2 Keep a sharp look out for booby-traps. The enemy never goes near them, so if you see them avoiding a particular spot, chances are that it is booby-trapped.
3 The first thing to do is to find the explosives. Go down and right to do this. Now go down and left to find the bridge and blow it up!
4 Try to make a map as you go along.
5 Use a quick-fire joystick if you can – it makes things a lot easier.

## REMARKS

A very good game. The blend of action and strategy, combined with superb presentation, make it a true winner.

## COMMENTS

JON: Great!

PRISONER OF WAR™

| 7 | 2 | | | 7–17 | 1 |
|---|---|---|---|------|---|

## REVIEW

A standard Beat 'em Up set in a jungle POW camp. You start with 3 lives and earn a bonus life for each 30,000 points scored. There are 4 levels to brawl through with the usual end-of-level guardians.

## WEAPONS

The only weapon you start with is your own body. Use it to **punch, kick** and **jump**. Along the way you can pick up the following, and you will need them: **brass knuckles** double the damage inflicted by punches; the **knife** can be used to stab or throw – once thrown the weapon is lost; a **grenade** is useful for larger enemies; the **machine-gun** appears as a 'G' symbol and is very powerful, but only has 10 bullets.

## SPECIALS

There are a few other special items to be collected. These include: **bullet proof vest** that appears as an 'A' symbol on screen and will reduce damage until you lose a life; **extra life** which appears as an 'L' symbol.

## THE ENEMY

You start off with rather stupid unarmed guards, but rapidly progress through the Knife then machine-gun armed enemies – the game calls them *Goons*. Later on there are *helicopters* – you need to have a gun or grenade by the time these appear.

## HINTS

1 Do not get too close to the enemy, your punches and kicks will not hit them.
2 Weapons can be picked up from dead guards.
3 Jump and then kick to take out motorcycles.
4 During the opening screen, press A B B UP UP DOWN LEFT – and you will earn 20 free lives.

## REMARKS

Double Dragon with palm trees.

RAMBO™

   6      2    7–70             1

## REVIEW

The game of the film. All-American hero shoots lots of commies and rescues his buddies. You play the Rambo character on a mission to rescue some POWs from the wicked commies. Between you and your goal are numerous nasties and buckets of add-on weapons. You have 3 lives and little else!

## WEAPONS

You start with a **combat knife**. Other weapons soon become available along the way. The **bow and arrow** is a good weapon with a decent range. The **throwing knife** is good for hand-to-hand fighting but a little short on range. The **exploding arrow** is twice as powerful as an ordinary arrow. The **machine-gun** is the business, while the **hand grenade** is powerful but only short-ranged.

## SPECIALS

**Medicine bottles** – drink these as you find them to replace lost energy.

## THE ENEMY

As well as the usual enemy soldiers, our hero also has to contend with a number of wild animals and a number of truly bizarre fantasy beasts. These include *Zombies* and *Ghosts*, who do not appear often, but watch out when they do! There are also 7 end-of-level guardians, each with its own special powers.

## HINTS

1 If you want to use the 'Transfer Points' mentioned in the manual, look out for the small 'N' and 'S' symbols that appear on the screen from time to time and then press the Up arrow.
2 Make maps of the various areas you visit as it is easy to get lost.
3 Unlike a lot of games, you have to fight almost everything to get the best out of the game.

## REMARKS

Not a bad game at all! Don't be put off by the Rambo theme.

### COMMENTS

Extremely violent – unnecessarily so.
THAT'S A SHAME: Calling the game Rambo!

# RC PRO-AM™

9      4      7–70      1

## REVIEW

This is a really neat idea; instead of a real car you control a radio-controlled model! Rather than the more normal view (up and behind), you view the action just as you would if you were driving the real thing (three-quarter perspective). The action is fast and furious, and the sound effects are great. The computer controls your three opponents, and for violence fans there's the added bonus of miniature missiles to blow the opposition away – GREAT!!

## WEAPONS

**Missiles** that are forward-firing and powerful, with a decent range. There are also delayed-action **bombs** – drop them as you go round and give the chasing cars a real surprise! You have neither weapons at the start, but can pick them up as you go.

## SPECIALS

Every now and again, you will see a letter appear on the screen. Drive over enough of these to spell out 'NINTENDO' and you'll be given a souped-up supercar to drive. You will also get the chance to customize your car at the end of each race. How much depends on how well you did in the last race. The better your position the more power-ups you'll get!

## THE ENEMY

The computer-controlled cars are smart, though fortunately they remain unarmed.

## HINTS

1 Save your weapons for really critical situations. The supply of them is extremely limited.
2 You can only carry one weapon at a time, so think before picking one up.
3 Try to avoid touching the sides of the track as this can slow you down a great deal.

**4** Keep your eyes open! The first few races are fairly straightforward, but later on all kinds of nasty traps begin to appear on the course.

## REMARKS

This is a great game. It may appear a little simplistic but there really are hours of fun to be had – buy it!

## COMMENTS

NIGEL: Brilliant – almost as good as the real thing.
THAT'S NICE: All round great game.

RENEGADE™

    6        2      7–17    1–2

## REVIEW

Standard Beat 'em Up format played out in a US subway. You start the game with only 1 life and there are 3 levels of difficulty.

## WEAPONS

Just the usual **kicks** and **punches** to start with. As you go through the game you will come across a number of 'P' symbols. Collect these and your kicks will be very powerful for a short while.

## SPECIALS

**Hamburgers** restore your power level to full. The **heart** brings in a friend to help you out, but he only stays for a short time. The 'S' symbol for **speed** makes you move very quickly, but again only for a short while.

## THE ENEMY

All the usual villains.

## HINTS

**1** Don't let the enemy get behind you – not only do they do a lot of damage but one may grab hold of you while another hits you!
**2** The only way to get any Specials is to use the 'Sit on Punch'.

## REMARKS

A very ordinary Beat 'em Up.

7    2    7–70    1

## REVIEW

A game in the mould of 'Knight Rider'. You drive a car and shoot things, but there is no story as such, just action. One interesting feature is the scoring system: each time you destroy a target with a single shot, you are awarded a multiplier to your score. This multiplier increases up to a maximum of 10. Scores achieved can therefore be increased by ten-fold. This bonus is removed as soon as the player misses a target.

The game has a total of 50 circuits or levels for you to complete and it is possible to continue the game three times before having to go back to the start. You start each game with the usual 3 lives.

## WEAPONS

Your standard weapon is the **machine-gun**, firing forward. However, there are a number of special weapons that can be picked up from the support jet as it flies overhead: the **Cruise Missile** destroys everything in front of you and comes with 3 reloads; the **UZ Cannon** is fully automatic with unlimited ammo – very useful.

## SPECIALS

These are collected in a similar way to the extra weapons. The **Electro Shield** makes you temporarily invulnerable to enemy attacks and can be used 3 times. **Nitro** goes F..A..S..T!! and also can be used 3 times.

## THE ENEMY

All the usual nasties you'd expect in a game like this. Watch out though for *land mines* and the *gun turrets* at the side of the road. Fortunately, everyone on the road is a bad guy.

## HINTS

1 Try to shoot carefully. Building up a good score multiplier is essential for decent scores.
2 Keep a eye on the Mine Indicator on the dashboard.

## REMARKS

A rather ordinary game of its type. There is absolutely nothing wrong with it, but sadly that is not quite enough these days.

## COMMENTS

NIGEL: I like Race 'em Ups. This is OK but check out Knight Rider first.

ROBOCOP™

7        3        7–70        1

## REVIEW

Film tie-in games often leave a little to be desired but not here. Robocop is a real peach and captures all of the excitement of its larger brother in the arcades. The game has our hero progressing through 6 sections of horizontally scrolling action. Each level has the usual end-of-level guardian to contend with. You start with 3 lives and 3 Continue options that are renewed each time you finish a level.

## WEAPONS

Robo has two basic weapons to start game: the **Auto-9 Hand Gun** is a very effective hand gun and comes with unlimited ammo; and the **punch** – some enemies can only be harmed by punching them and a small indicator light prompts this action when in range. In addition, there are two more guns that can be picked up along the way: the **machine-gun**, is very useful because of its automatic fire, but be warned, there are only 50 rounds of ammo; the **Cobra Assault Cannon** is ultra-powerful but very limited on ammo – however, it will come in handy for the end-of-level guardians.

## SPECIALS

**Battery Rechargers** give you more time to complete a level, and **Power Food** restores Robo's lost energy.

## THE ENEMY

Various 'crims'; they shoot at you, throw things, try to beat you up and even ride motorcycles into you.

## HINTS

**1** Watch your on-screen detectors.

**2** When in Infra Red mode, look for the part of the screen that is flashing – that is where the enemy is.

**3** Always keep an eye on the 'Punch' indicator.

**4** End-of-level guardians all have their vulnerable spots. Try experimenting rather than just blasting away.

## REMARKS

A very good game of its type.

## COMMENTS

NIGEL: I spent a lot of money in the arcades on this one and never got anywhere. I still can't get anywhere with this version but at least its cheaper!

RUSH 'N' ATTACK™

      7      3     7–70          1

## REVIEW

One of the newer horizontal Beat 'em Ups to come out on Nintendo, and another game transferred from the arcades. This is a fairly standard game that benefits from superb presentation.

## WEAPONS

Bucket loads. Although you only start with a weedy knife, you won't have to put up with it for long. The **bazooka** is particularly nifty.

## SPECIALS

Everything you'd expect in a game like this.

## THE ENEMY

Loads of the stereotype commies you'd expect. They are real people and die by the hundreds! There are also a fair number of tanks, planes etc, that can prove really tough if you haven't got the right weapon.

## HINTS

**1** Learn the patterns; they are very obvious after a while.

**2** The Autogiros at the end of level 4 can be beaten in the following way. Wait for them near the left hand side of the screen, dodging any grenades that come your way. Then, as they fly towards you, jump up and kill them with your knife . . . simple really!

**3** If you can run from paratroopers, move to the left of the screen. As they descend, move slowly to the right and let their bullets fly over your head. Once you are on the right hand side of the screen, let them have it with everything you've got!

**4** To destroy the secret weapon at the end, you need a bazooka. If you have not got one, do not despair. There are several soldiers that have!

## COMMENTS

THAT'S A SHAME: Again, too much violence.

SKYSHARK™

    8       2     7–70    1–2

## REVIEW

An aircraft-based Shoot 'em Up. You find yourself at the controls of a vintage World War II P40, or Tiger Shark fighter aircraft. The game is a basic vertical scrolling affair that puts both ground and air-based enemies up against you. The action is fast and furious, and the overall level of graphics is excellent.

At the start you have 4 lives. For each 50,000 points scored, you get an extra life.

## WEAPONS

The Shark has two basic weapons: the **cannon** engage flying enemies and fire forwards; and the **bombs** can be used against ground targets – they pack more punch than cannon but are limited in number and more difficult to aim.

## SPECIALS

After certain ground targets are destroyed, a 'B' will appear on the screen, fly over this and a bonus bomb will be given to you. Shooting an entire wave of *RED* enemy fighters will produce an 'S' symbol on screen. Flying over this will add progressively to your Shark's abilities. These are lost when you are destroyed.

## THE ENEMY

Just about every kind of World War II enemy you can think off: planes of all sizes, as well as tanks, anti-aircraft guns and ships.

## HINTS

1 Watch out for tanks hiding in trees!
2 Save bombs for larger ground targets.
3 Bombs can be used to deflect bullets when you are in real trouble.

## REMARKS

Another Shoot 'em Up very much in the mould of '1943'. A fun, if not particularly original, game.

## COMMENTS

NIGEL: I prefer '1943'!
THAT'S NICE: Excellent graphics.
THAT'S A SHAME: Very unoriginal idea.

SPY VS. SPY™

| 3 | 9 | 7–70 | 1–2 |

## REVIEW

A game like Spy Vs. Spy does not fall into any of the categories normally associated with video games. It is based on the antics of two spies made famous by *MAD* comic. The action is shown in split screen, so both spies can be seen at the same time. You have to locate secret papers and then escape to the airport within a set time. As usual, there are a few complications along the way.

What makes this game so much fun is the other spy. Controlled either by the console or another player, he is trying to achieve the same thing as you. To further complicate matters, both of you can set traps that will delay any spy unlucky enough to get caught in them. The game has 8 levels or complexes to explore.

## WEAPONS

Not so much weapons as traps! **Buckets of water** are placed on the top of doors. **Dynamite** is hidden in a drawer or behind a picture. **Springs** are used in the same way as dynamite, though they are not quite as effective. **Time bombs** can be placed anywhere, and they go off after a set time.

## SPECIALS

As well as the secret papers that are your prime objective there are also a number of other useful items to be found. **Umbrellas** guard against the effects of the water bucket. As well as being used for the water bucket trap **water buckets** can be used to disarm the dynamite. **Wire cutters** disarm the Giant Spring and are found in the wall-mounted tool boxes.

## THE ENEMY

The enemy spy is very good at his job. Don't expect an easy ride when the console is controlling him.

## HINTS

**1** Before trying to leave, you must have a briefcase, a set of keys, money and a passport in addition to the secret papers.

**2** Try to avoid meeting the other spy. Fisticuffs will inevitably follow and that can be a real nuisance.

**3** Think carefully about positioning your traps. Try to remember where they are since they will hurt you if you happen to trigger them by accident.

## REMARKS

A truly excellent game that is a must for any Nintendo owner with half a brain.

## COMMENTS

NIGEL: Love it!
JON: That's because he's only got half a brain!
THAT'S NICE: Just about everything.
THAT'S A SHAME: Nothing as far as we can see.

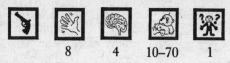

8      4     10–70    1

## REVIEW

Star Voyager, while unquestionably falling into the Shoot 'em Up category, also has many features of a flight simulator. The scenario is the standard one – a lone spaceship against hordes of aliens. You are the last thing between us and oblivion. There are 8 galaxies to clear.

## WEAPONS

Your ship comes armed with a fairly ordinary **laser gun** which fires forward. The ship can also sustain a fair amount of damage before it is destroyed.

## SPECIALS

Docking at the **Base Station** allows repairs and refuelling. Landing on the **Monolith** will give you a Hyperdrive Engine to go anywhere without worrying about fuel. Landing on the **Planets** can provide a number of goodies, including a super-smart bomb and an extremely powerful add-on super-laser.

## THE ENEMY

Hordes of enemy ships of various sizes form the bulk of the enemy, along with the occasional Mother Ship. There are also a number of 'natural' hazards to contend with, including *Black Holes* – don't go anywhere near these!; *Asteroids* – steer carefully around these; and *Space Streams* – powerful currents that can seriously alter your course.

## HINTS

1 Keep an eye on your Information Screen.
2 Be careful when using the Hyperdrive. Only being a fraction off-course can be a real pain.

## REMARKS

A really challenging game that requires a considerable amount of thought, as well as simple blasting to win. The complexity of controls will put off some people.

## COMMENTS

NIGEL: Looks like a winner.

### STRIDER™

8    2    7–70    1

## REVIEW

A bionic superhero is dropped deep in the heart of Russia with instructions to cause general mayhem.

## WEAPONS

Strider's only basic weapon is the ability to **punch** and **kick** the enemy.

## SPECIALS

**Yellow Attack Boots** give super kick attacks. **Blue Aqua Boots** allow Strider to walk on water. **Red Magnet Boots** let our hero climb up some walls. As well as these weapons, you can pick up a selection of special weaponry and tricks. Once collected, these can be accessed via the Status Screen.

## THE ENEMY

Loads of the normal Beat 'em Up fodder, liberally sprinkled with extra hard types just to make things interesting.

## HINTS

1 Not all enemies need to be fought. Try jumping over them!
2 Keep a look-out for keys. Without these, some parts of the game cannot be reached.

## REMARKS

Oh no, not another Beat 'em Up! That said, Strider is a perfectly good game if you like that sort of thing.

# SUPER MARIO BROS.<sup>TM</sup>

    8       5     7–16    1–2

## REVIEW

Super Mario Bros. is perhaps the most famous game in the entire history of the genre. The game revolves around the brothers' attempt to rescue the Mushroom King's daughter from the evil Turtles. The game progresses through a huge cutesie panorama of bizarre enemies, with numerous specials and puzzles galore. In all, there are 8 multi-screen worlds with 4 levels in each to explore and you have 3 lives to start with.

## WEAPONS

None to start with, but you can **run** and **jump**! Later on, pick up a **Fire Flower** and begin to lob **fire balls** at people.

## SPECIALS

There are lots of these. **1 up mushrooms** give you extra life. The **axe** is good for getting rid of Bowser, the arch-villain of the game. The **Fire Flower** gives the Bros. the ability to use fire balls. Bounce and bounce and bounce on the **trampoline**. **Coins** are scattered about all over the place – 100 of them will buy you an extra life. **Magic mushrooms** give the Bros. super-jumping abilities. **Starman** makes the Bros. invincible, but only for a short period!

## THE ENEMY

The *Beetle* is fast; fire balls are useless against him, but jumping on him does the trick! *Bill* is slow but packs a long-range punch; try to attack him from above or behind. *Bloopers* are like jellyfish – slow and dumb. Fire Balls will get rid of them easily. *Bowser* is the arch-villain. A dozen fire balls or the axe will do the job on him. *Flying Fish* are tough – try jumping on them. *Kooper Troopers* are enemy turtles. Jump on them and then put the boot in. They come in several colours and the green

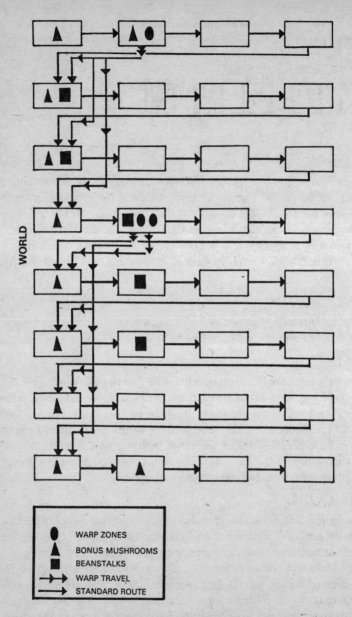

WORLD

WARP ZONES
BONUS MUSHROOMS
BEANSTALKS
WARP TRAVEL
STANDARD ROUTE

**MARIO BROS. SHORTCUT**

100

ones seem to be the hardest. *Lakitu* is a high-flying bird, and it drops nasty eggs on you. *Little Goomba* is a traitor mushroom – squash him!!! *Pirana Plants* lurk in flowerpots. Avoid them, or use a fire ball *Podoboo* is Bowser's bodyguard.

## HINTS

**1** Try standing on the tops of drainpipes; interesting things can happen.

**2** Practise the running jump. It's an absolute must.

**3** Coins are hidden all over the place. Be thorough in your searches.

**4** A number of 'warp zones' exist in the game that allow you to take short cuts to different parts of the game. Look for the ones in World 1, Level 2 and World 4, Level 2.

**5** There are 1-up mushrooms hidden just before the chasm in World 1, Level 1 and another above the bridge in World 3, Level 1.

**6** At the end of World 3, Level 1 you will come across a pyramid. Hang around here and a Kooper Trooper will appear. Jump on his shell for an extra life.

## REMARKS

What a great game! This is a must for everyone's collection.

## SUPER MARIO BROS. 2™

     8          6        7–16     1–2

## REVIEW

The Mario Bros. are back! The people of Subcon, a land of dreams, have fallen under the evil spell of the infamous Wart and only the Bros. can save them. This game is much more of an adventure than the first, with more puzzles and much more thought required.

There are 7 multi-level worlds and you have 3 lives to start with. A very nice touch is the ability to pick one of four characters with which to play. As well as the two Bros. you can also play Princess Toadstool, or a Toad. Both of these have different strengths and weaknesses.

## WEAPONS

Just **punching** and the ability to **jump** up and down on things! Later on you'll be able to pick up **bombs**. Throwing these at the enemy or walls will have a dramatic effect!

## SPECIALS

Even more of these than in the first Bros. epic. **1-ups** give you an extra life, and **bombs** go off with a bang! Collect 100 **coins** for an extra life. Collect **cherries** to bring in the Starman. The **flying carpet** belongs to Pidgit (see the Enemy). Jump onto the carpet as it passes and throw him off; the carpet is then yours! **Grass** replaces lost energy, while **magic potions** cast useful spells. **Mushrooms** increase your life energy. **POW** is a Mega-screen blasting earthquake. The **rocket** is well-hidden, but can zoom you to another part of the game if you find it – try looking under the grass. **Secret rooms** are hidden under jars, and the **Starman** makes you invincible for a short time. The **stopwatch** temporarily freezes the enemy, and appears with every fifth vegetable that you pick. Throw the **turtle shells** and **vegetables** at the bad guys!

## THE ENEMY

*Albatross* drops bombs – dodge them at all costs. *Beezo* is another flyer; red ones divebomb you, pink ones fly straight and level. *Birdo* is a minor guardian and a real nuisance. Throw the eggs at him – 3 hits and he's out. *Bob-Omb* throws bombs at you! *Claw Grip* is nasty but slow, while *Flurry* is fast, but only found in cold places. *Fryguy* spits fire, but is only found in hot places. Three bombs will see the *Mouser* off. *Panser* is an innocent-looking plant that spits fire if you get too close. *Phanto* chases after you if you manage to find a key. Try dropping the key for a while to confuse him, but remember to pick it up again! Pinch *Pidgit's* flying carpet! *Pokey* is covered in spikes – don't try to pick him up! *Shyguys* are numerous but weak. *Snifits* are innocent-looking, but they spit bullets. *Sparks* are only found underground – beware the lightning bolts he throws. *Tryclyde* is very hard; throw lots of POW blocks and hope for the best! *Wart* is the chief bad guy and found on level 7.

## HINTS

1 Master the art of running and jumping at the same time.

**2** There's a warp zone on the other side of the waterfall on World 1, Level 1.

**3** The slot machine is predictable. Once you get in the rhythm you can win a life nearly every go.

**4** Even though it might look impossible, most baddies can be jumped on and thrown, regardless of their size.

## REMARKS

Another brilliant game in the Mario Bros. series.

THAT'S A SHAME: With only two Continues available, you'll probably have to restart many times.

### TEENAGE MUTANT NINJA TURTLES™

| 8 | 3 | 7–70 | 1 |

## REVIEW

The plot line is standard stuff, with the Evil Shredder kidnapping April, the Turtles' friendly reporter. During the adventure you can control any of the Turtles, but may only use one at a time. The game is beautifully presented with outstanding graphics.

## WEAPONS

Each Turtle starts the game armed with a different weapon:

Leonardo: **Sword** (Katana, to give it its original Japanese name)

Raphael: **Sai**

Michaelangelo: **Nunchuckus**

Donatello: **Bo Staff.**

During the game there are opportunities to acquire other weapons: the **boomerang** is a powerful thrown weapon – it returns after being thrown but you have to catch it, which can be a bit tricky; and **Shuriken**, metal stars, can also be thrown, but these don't come back.

## SPECIALS

**Pizza** – watch out for this stuff scattered around the game. It replenishes some of the Turtles' lost energy.

## THE ENEMY

*Shredder* is the main bad guy, but you won't meet him until you are well into the game. Unfortunately, he has the ability to turn ordinary folk into crazed maniacs, so just about everything you meet is likely to be an enemy!

## HINTS

1 Use the ladders quickly. When you are on one you are defenceless.
2 Get used to swapping between characters.
3 The sleeping soldiers can be killed very easily as long as you stand exactly the right distance away from them and then take a swing!
4 When you find pizza at either the beginning or the end of a game you can keep re-entering that section and eat the same piece again and again!

## REMARKS

An excellent game with all round addictive appeal.

## COMMENTS

THAT'S A SHAME: Turtles just don't behave like this! Thank goodness!

TETRIS™

8      8      7–70    1–2

## REVIEW

As well as being an immensely popular game, Tetris is also incredibly difficult to describe! You get a screens'-worth of space at the start. 'Shapes' fall down from the top of the screen and have to be slotted together so that no space remains. Every time a row is filled in, that row is removed. The game ends when you cannot slot a piece in. A game as simple as this offers an almost infinite number of possibilities.

## THE ENEMY

We suppose that the shapes themselves could be considered enemies. They certainly are if you can't fit them in! On the whole they tend to appear more quickly and be more awkwardly shaped the further you progress.

## HINTS

1 Try to think ahead and keep an eye on the next piece all the time.

**2** Avoid leaving small or strangely shaped gaps.
**3** Think in three dimensions. Shapes *can* be rotated.
**4** Don't worry about your score to start with, just fill in those rows. There'll be plenty of time for fancy stuff later.

## REMARKS

Similar to Rubik's Cube. You'll either love it or hate it!

## COMMENTS

PAUL: Love it!
NIGEL: Hate it!
JON: See what I mean!

THUNDERCADE™

6      2      7–70      1–2

## REVIEW

Another arcade conversion. This game is for Shoot 'em Up die-hards only. The action is fast and furious, the enemy legion, the add-ons endless . . . There are 4 levels and you have 3 lives. You are riding a motorcycle and have a tactical bomber on call for tricky situations!

## WEAPONS

You start the game with your **motorcycle** and a single **machine-gun**. Throughout the game you will encounter numerous add-on weapons in the form of **sidecars**. Grab these as you go past. Be warned though – sidecars appear in random order and it is possible to pick up a lesser weapon than the one you already have!

## SPECIALS

As usual, simply drive over the symbols to collect them. **Bombs** boost your bomber. The **parachute** gives you 4 extra missiles. The **1-up** gives you an extra life.

## THE ENEMY

More than you can shake a stick at. Ranging from plants right up to jet fighters and everything else in between!

## HINTS

**1** Save the bomber for real emergencies.

**2** While you are flying the bomber you cannot be shot.

**3** Shoot carefully. At the end of each level you will be awarded a bonus for accuracy.

**4** To take out the final target (the nuclear power plant) you have to shoot all of the snipers at the windows.

**5** Once you have a powerful set of weapons, don't pick up any more – they may be worse than the ones you already have.

## REMARKS

A great Shoot 'em Up. Buy it.

## COMMENTS

JON: Love it!!!

THAT'S NICE: The bomber is a great twist.

### TIGER HELI™

| 9 | 2 | 7–70 | 1–2 |
| --- | --- | --- | --- |

## REVIEW

The Nintendo version of the arcade hit. You have to pilot a hi-tec super-chopper and blast just about everything in sight. The screen scrolls from top to bottom and is seen from overhead. The game play is very difficult and very fast – one for the experts! There are 4 levels in all and just 3 lives to start with.

## WEAPONS

An unlimited supply of **missiles** and two **super-bombs** start you off.

## SPECIALS

The **Red Cross** gives you another helicopter that flies alongside and fires missiles out to the side. The **Grey Cross** fires missiles out of the front. The **Green Cross** replenishes your stock of super-bombs.

You can carry up to 2 bombs at once and employ 2 support helicopters. If you already have them, shoot the crosses instead and get bonus points!

## THE ENEMY

Planes, trains and automobiles, and tanks and ships and ... and ... and ... everything you see on the screen!

## HINTS

1 To continue the game, press both the 'A' and 'B' buttons as the game ends.
2 Learn the patterns.
3 Try to keep about two-thirds of the way down the screen wherever possible. This gives you the best field of fire.
4 Beware of enemy sneaking up behind you.
5 Get a quick-fire joystick!

## REMARKS

Fast and furious, this is a real winner. Arcade freaks will have hours of fun.

UNCANNY X-MEN™

6        7        8–20      1–2

## REVIEW

Nice comic conversion with all your *Marvel* superheroes. Simple plot, but you have the chance to control any of the superheroes and change midway through the game (only in the 1-player version).

## WEAPONS

There are some useful special weapons. The **Force Shield** protects you for a while. The **Smart Bomb** clears the enemy from the screen. The **Stasis Bomb** freezes all the enemy for a while.

## SPECIALS

**Computer discs** – collect one every time you beat a mutant; and the **energy cell** restores your energy.

## THE ENEMY

There are lots of these, here are the top guys: *Magneto* – watch out for his bombs, they'll immobilize you; *Boomerang* – guess what he chucks;

107

*Juggernaut* is a magic user and nasty; and the *White Queen* is very tough.

## HINTS

Watch your energy level, and swap between your two X-Men to keep them up to full power.

## REMARKS

Nothing special – go for it if you like *Marvel* comics.

UNCLE FESTER'S QUEST™

   6      7    8–20   1–2

## REVIEW

Here they are, the Adams family. Uncle Fester tries to rescue the local townspeople from the clutches of marauding aliens, There are plenty of places to explore whilst listening to the bouncy music.

## WEAPONS

Blue **guns** boost your firepower, but avoid the red ones because they'll take it away! **Missiles** can KO loadsa baddies in one go, as can **TNT** – BOOOOM! **Whips** act just like the guns, blue increases fire power and red takes it away.

## SPECIALS

**Bulbs** have colours just like the guns and whips. **Invisible potions** make you invisible – no! **Keys** can be useful, and you need **money** to get a lovely scrummy hot dog. **Noose** calls Lurch. The **potion** is a great tonic. The **Vise Grip** should be used if you've been bitten by an insect.

## THE ENEMY

*Alien Bosses*, *Giant Scorpion* (don't tangle with this), *Globule*, *Skeeter* (the source of the mosquitoes), *Slime Replicators* (try not to hit them, they'll only multiply).

## HINTS

1 Use your whip at full strength against the Alien Bosses.
2 Draw a map.

**3** Your relatives have got some useful items.
**4** Get yourself a turbo-fire joystick.
**5** There's a hidden power-up in the dead end wall in the house off the path.
**6** Keep your gun charged to the limit. Don't fire at the balloons, whip them!

## REMARKS

High humour here! Some lovely three-dimensional work. Nice opening mini-story.

### WHO FRAMED ROGER RABBIT™

| 7 | 4 | 7–17 | 1 |

## REVIEW

An action adventure detective game. The game has an overhead view and a close-up side view.

## WEAPONS

None, but there are plenty of 'gags'.

## SPECIALS

Hundreds of them! **Baseballs, bombs, boxing gloves, bricks** (great for bashing snakes), **crowbar** (forget the key), **detonator, dynamite, exploding cigar, fishbone** (get rid of that cat), **fist, flashlight, meat** (distract animals with this), **password, portable, rose** (give to Jessica and get a clue), **six shooter, spring shoes** (jump over obstacles), **wallet** and **whistle** (calls Benny).

## ENEMY

Lots of humans and rodents!

## HINTS

**1** Make a map.
**2** Breaking down doors is OK, but move fast or Judge Doom will get you!

## REMARKS

Parents should be aware that, although this is meant for younger players, it is unlikely that they will be able to cope with the clues and information which is a shame.

ZELDA II: THE ADVENTURES OF LINK™

6      7      7–17      1

## REVIEW

Just like 'The Legend of Zelda', there are literally hundreds of monsters to fight, plus plenty of clues, characters, special powers and lots to explore! The ability to cast spells is useful, if not vital, as are the special objects (such as the hammer and the magic glove). As with the original, you can save your game and Continue as often as you want. Link restarts the game from the beginning and not from where he was killed, but you do get to keep all his booty. The quest? Well this time Link goes off in search of 6 crystals to place in 6 statues to awaken Princess Zelda.

## WEAPONS

A great selection – from the standard **sword** to the more exotic . . . well, find out for yourself!

## SPECIALS

There are so many specials we have decided to give you some guidance about how to find and use them. Decipher the clues and search thoroughly; Hyrule is huge, if you search blindly it would take weeks. To make any progress you need to find clues and follow them. Combat is trial and error to begin with, at least until you know the enemy, but try different tactics and use different spells.

## ENEMIES

Here are some tips on how to deal with some of the baddies. The *Stalfos* are fairly weak-kneed. To beat the *Ironknuckles*, jump up and hit them on the head; pressing forward and swinging at the same time for the best effect! Fire will always damage the monsters that your sword won't. When you fight your own shadow at the end of the game, hit it through its shield. If your life force is at full strength, throw your sword – it is much safer! The *Bits* that attack you on the plain outside the castle where Zelda is sleeping give you a great opportunity to boost your points. Two Bits will appear on one side of the screen and three on the other. By going back and forth you can collect plenty of points to help boost your life, attacking skills and magic. Use jumping and shield spells against the guardian of the first palace, and you can get rid of the spider by blowing the flute.

## HINTS

1 The magic glove can be found in the second palace.

2 To reach the island palace you must fall through a hole in the cemetery.

3 There are hidden pits in the Great Palace. Sometimes it's worth going down them. One is well hidden under a pile of rocks.

4 Explore the forest, the desert and the swamp. They are packed with hidden objects. Special bonus – there's a 1-UP hidden in the desert near the graveyard. Always enter squares that look different from those nearby.

5 Always go back to the towns after taking a palace or grabbing a magic object. The villagers may have something else to say to you.

6 The magic hammer is *not* in the swamp, it is in a cave.

7 Hit statues inside palaces for magical boosts. Some might come to life and attack you!

8 The water is a maze.

9 Boots let you walk on water.

10 If you don't have a key, use the fairy spell.

## REMARKS

Great game, with absolutely hours and hours of enjoyment. Progress really depends on you and your wits.

## COMMENTS

JON: Better than the original?

PAUL: True, but without the hints progress is very slow.

NIGEL: Just as well I sussed them all out!

# SHORT REVIEWS

During our research there were quite a few games we came across that for one reason or another did not merit a section of their own, either because they were rubbish, not released outside the USA yet, or simply because they were so new that we did not have enough info for a full review.

## ALTERED BEAST[TM]

Another arcade conversion and likely to be quite a success. Very similar to the well-known 'Ghosts and Goblins'. Watch out for the lions and wolves. You can only hurt these by kicking them!

## ARCHON[TM]

A cross between chess and an arcade Beat 'em Up. We are told it is a real laugh.

## GHOSTS AND GOBLINS[TM]

Quite an old game but only just finding its way into the UK. The patterns in this game are very predictable. Spend as little time on ladders as you can – you are vulnerable there and you can't fire back.

## GOONIES[TM]

A dull game based on a dull film. It is unlikely that it will ever be released in the UK. If you do get to play it, try this cheat out for size: type in the code SUG NY4W T!NUU!UF to get all the equipment you need.

## GUARDIAN LEGEND[TM]

Try using the password VQuM uMDM oouk 4cuK iUS3 D5gI 4yFG!

112

## GUERILLA WAR™

A very nasty horizontal Shoot 'em Up with extreme violence. The game is OK but unsuitable for younger children. It also suffers from being far too easy.

## HOOPS™

A one or two-player basketball sim that is very popular in the USA, but not available in the UK yet. Excellent if you can get hold of a copy that works on the UK system.

## INFILTRATOR™

Fly super helicopter! Get chased a lot! Get out of helicopter and kill lots of people! That's all we know. Looks like this one is a definite for Bad Taste since poison gas plays an important part in the combat!

## JACKAL™

When playing this game, running over soldiers is just as good as shooting them. Grenades can be thrown over walls. Don't try and shoot the lasers at Checkpoint Charlie, just run! Try to avoid the water as it slows you down. Giant helicopters need several direct hits with grenades to destroy them and watch out for the landmines near Checkpoint Tango.

## MAGIC OF SCHEHERAZADE

Zelda meets the horizontally scrolling cutesie and apparently has a ball. Take time to listen to the townspeople, and note that wise men have spells. Try out these naughty passwords – 1W, 2W, 3W, 4W, 5W – then press Enter. We think you'll like the result.

## MIKE TYSON'S PUNCH-OUT™

Standard boxing sim, more technique than tips, but try this against Piston Honda. When he blinks, put up your guard. He will lower his and you can punch him in the face.

## NOBUNGA'S AMBITION^TM

An immensely complex wargame set in feudal Japan. Sadly not released in the UK yet. This isn't going to be the sort of game for glib little hints and tips! Buy it as soon as you can, but we'll be there first!

## QIX

An odd little game where you control a line! You must use the line to make boxes and then paint them. Also on the screen are a number of baddies who will kill you if yo are caught in mid-draw! Very addictive but only one hint: draw lots of small boxes rather than a few big ones!

## R TYPE^TM

A vastly popular, but overrated horizontally scrolling Shoot 'em Up. Although very pretty, the patterns are again predictable. Learn them and you've all but won.

## SEVEN TWENTY DEGREES^TM

Skate-boarding. A good game with a selection of different courses and a host of 'go-faster' extras. Worth a look!

## SIMON'S QUEST^TM

A horizontally scrolling Beat 'em Up with a fantasy theme. Collect magic items and beat the pink stuff out of the baddies. If you've played Castlevania and enjoyed it then this one might be for you. If you haven't then buy Castlevania instead.

## SOLOMON'S KEY^TM

A sweet little arcade adventure that sees you mooching around a mine. In a nutshell, it is about manipulating blocks and killing things. Starts off easy and gets very hard, very quickly!

## TOP GUN^TM

The Nintendo version of the arcade hit. All you have to do for the first 30,000 miles is to keep the controller pressed up! Apparently you avoid all the missiles this way, which seems like duff programming to us.

## TRACK AND FIELD™

The Olympic sports sim arrives on the Nintendo. There are 12 different events and all of them pretty good. A must for sim fans!

## TROJAN™

When you die, press UP and START simultaneously and you'll continue on the last stage that you reached. On the second part of stage two, you'll find an extra life. To get to it, go to the end of the lake and start whacking about with your sword.

## TWIN COBRA™

Guess what? You're flying that helicopter again. You shoot things and pick up lots of super add-ons. Unoriginal, but a perfectly workperson-like Shoot 'em Up.

## WIZARDS & WARRIORS™

A classic, a bit old now though. You'll need Lava Boots to survive Fire World. The exist key to the Red Caves is on the ledge at the top of the screen. To get the pink key, jump to the left as you climb up, or when you get to the pink door, run to the edge and jump off the left side. You will fall through the air and land on the key! From the second forest scene, just past the red caves, go all the way left. Jump up repeatedly using the UP arrow, Kuros will disappear from the left side and reappear on the right much further into the game.

California Games is a trademark of Epyx, Inc. © 1987 Epyx, Inc. MB and Milton Bradley are trademarks of Milton Bradley Corp. Game pak © 1988 Milton Bradley Company.

Castlevania II: Simons Quest is a trademark of Konami Industry Co. Ltd. © 1989 Konami Industry Co. Ltd.

City Connection is a trademark of Jaleco USA © 1988 Jaleco USA.

Clash at Demonhead is a trademark of Vic Tokai, Inc. © 1989 Vic Tokai, Inc.

Cobra Triangle is a trademark of Nintendo of America Inc. © 1988 Nintendo of America Inc.

Contra is a trademark of Konami Industry Co. Ltd. © 1988 Konami Industry Co. Ltd.

Cybernoid is a trademark of Gremlin Graphics, Inc. Licensed to Acclaim Entertainment, Inc. © 1989 Acclaim Entertainment, Inc.

Desert Commander is a trademark of Kemco. © 1989 Kemco.

Donkey Kong, Donkey Kong Junior, Donkey Kong II, Donkey Kong Math, are trademarks of Nintendo of America, Inc. © 1988 Nintendo of America, Inc.

Double Dragon is a trademark of Technos Japan Corp. © 1988 Technos Japan Corp. Game pak © 1988 Tradewest, Inc.

Double Dragon II: The Revenge is copyright Technos Japan, Inc. © 1989. Double Dragon II: Game pak is a trademark of Acclaim Entertainment, Inc. © 1989 Acclaim Entertainment, Inc.

Double Dribble is a trademark of Konami Industry Ltd. © 1989 Konami Industry Ltd.

Duck Hunt is a trademark of Nintendo of America, Inc. © 1987 Nintendo of America, Inc.

DuckTales and Capcom are trademarks of Capcom USA, Inc. Characters © 1989 Walt Disney Co. Game pak © 1989 Capcom USA, Inc.

Excitebike is a trademark of Nintendo of America, Inc. © 1989 Nintendo of America, Inc.

Fist of the North Star is a trademark of Bronson, Tetsuo Hara/Shueisha, Fuji TV, Toei Animation. © 1987 Toei Animation, Shouei System. Game pk © 1988, Taxan USA Corp.

Flying Dragon: The Secret Scroll is a trademark of Culture Brain, Inc. © 1988 Culture Brain, Inc.

Friday the 13th game pak © 1988 LJN Toys Ltd. The Friday the 13th logo is a trademark of Paramount Pictures Corp. © 1988 Paramount Pictures Corp. Enteractive is a trademark of LJN Toys, Ltd.

Gauntlet is a registered trademark of Atari Games Corp., © 1985 Atari Games Corp.

Ghosts and Goblins is a trademark of Capcom USA, Inc. © 1987 Capcom USA, Inc.

GOLGO 13 is a trademark of Vic Tokai, Inc./Saito Pro. © 1988 Vic Tokai, Inc./Saito Pro.

Goonies is a trademark of Warner Bros. Licensed to Konami Industry Co. Ltd. © 1988 Warner Bros. Inc.

The Guardian Legend is a trademark of Irem Corp. Broderbund is a trademark of Broderbund Software, Inc. © 1988 Irem Corp., Compile and Broderbund Software, Inc.

117

Guerrilla War is a trademark of SNK Corporation of America. Game pak © 1989 SNK Corporation of America.

Hoops is a trademark of Jaleco USA Inc. © 1989 Jaleco USA Inc.

Ikari Warriors is a trademark of SNK Corp. of America. © 1987 SNK Corp. of America.

Ikari Warriors II: Victory Road is a trademark of SNK Corp. of America. © 1988 SNK Corp.

Infiltrator program contents © 1989, 1986 Gray Matter. Licensed to Mindscape, Inc. Game pak © 1989 Mindscape, Inc.

Ironsword: Wizards & Warriors II and Kuros are trademarks of Acclaim Entertainment, Inc. Wizards & Warriors © 1987 Rare, Ltd. Game pak © 1987 Acclaim Entertainment, Inc.

Jackal is a trademark of Konami Industry Co. Ltd. © 1988 Konami Industry Co. Ltd.

John Elway's Quarterback © Tradewest, Inc.

Jordan vs. Bird: One on One is a trademark of Electronic Arts. © 1989 Milton Bradley Company.

Karnov is a trademark of Data East USA © 1989 Data East USA.

Kid Kool is a trademark of Vic Tokai. © 1989 Vic Tokai.

Kid Niki, Radical Ninja is a trademark of Data East USA, Inc., © 1987 Data East USA, Inc. Manufactured under license from Irem Corp.

Knight Rider is a trademark of Universal City Studios, Inc. © 1982 Universal City Studios, Inc. licensed to Acclaim Entertainment, Inc. © 1989 Acclaim Entertainment, Inc.

Kung-Fu Heroes in a trademark of Culture Brain USA, Inc. © 1988 Culture Brain USA, Inc.

Lee Trevino's Fighting Golf is a trademark of SNK Corporation of America © 1989 SNK Corporation of America.

Legacy of the Wizard is a trademark of Broderbund Software, Inc. © 1987 and 1988, Falcom. © 1988 Broderbund Software, Inc.

Legendary Wings is a trademark of Capcom USA, Inc. © 1987 Capcom USA, Inc.

The Legend of Zelda, Nintendo, and Zelda are trademarks of Nintendo of America, Inc. © 1986, 1987 Nintendo of America, Inc.

The Magic of Scheherazade is a trademark of Culture Brain USA. © 1989 Culture Brain USA.

Mappy-Land is a trademark of Namco Ltd. © 1983/1988 Namco.

Marble Madness is a registered trademark of Atari Games Corp. © 1988 Tengen. Game pak © 1988 Milton Bradley Company.

Mega Man 2 is a trademark of Capcom USA, Inc. Capcom is a registered trademark of Capcom USA, Inc. © 1988 and 1989 Capcom USA, Inc.

Metal Gear is a trademark of Ultra Software Corporation. © 1988 Ultra Software Corporation.

Mike Tyson's Punch-Out is a trademark of Nintendo of America. Inc. © 1989 Nintendo of America, Inc.

Milon's Secret Castle is a trademark of Hudson Soft USA, Inc. © 1987 Hudson Soft USA, Inc.

Mickey's Mousecapade is a trademark of Capcom USA, Inc. Characters © 1988 Walt Disney Co. Game pak © 1988 Capcom USA, Inc.

The game pak NFL Football is a trademark of LJN Toys, Ltd. © 1988 LJN Toys, Ltd. NFL and the NFL shield are trademarks of the National Football League.

Nobunga's Ambition is a registered trademark of Koei Corp. © 1989 Koei Corp.

Operation Wolf and Taito are trademarks of Taito America Corp. Operation Wolf © 1988 Taito America Corp.

Pac Man is a trademark of Tengen Inc. © 1988 Tengen Inc.

Phantom Fighter and FCI are trademarks of Judisankei Communications Intl., Inc. Phantom Fighter © 1989 Fujisankei Communications Intl., Inc.

Platoon is a trademark of 1986 Helmdale Film Corporation. Software rights and game design sublicensed from Ocean Software Limited. Game pak © 1988 Sun Corporation of America.

P.O.W. and Prisoners of War are trademarks of SNK Corp. of America. © 1989 SNK Corp. of America.

RC Pro-Am is a trademark of Nintendo of America, Inc. © 1989 Nintendo of America, Inc.

Rambo is a registered trademark of Carolco. © 1985 and 1988 Carolco. Game pak © 1988 Acclaim Entertainment, Inc.

Renegade is a registered trademark of Taito Software, Inc. Renegade © 1987 Taito Software, Inc.

Road Blasters is a trademark of Tengen, Inc. © 1986, 1989 Tengen, Inc. Licensed to Mindscape, Inc. Mindscape is a trademark of Minscape, Inc. Game pak © 1989 Mindscape, Inc.

Robocop is a trademark of Orion Pictures Corporation, © 1987 Orion Pictures Corp. Game pak © 1988 Data East USA, Inc.

R Type is a trademark of Ire © 1989 Ire.

Rush 'n' Attack is a trademark of Konami Industry Co. Ltd. © 1987 Konami Inudstry Co. Ltd.

Sky Shark is a trademark of Taito America Corp. © 1988 Taito America Corp.

Solomon's Key is a trademark of Temco © 1988 Temco.

Spy vs. Spy and Mad are registered trademarks of E.C. Publication, Inc. Simulvision, Simulplay and First Star Software are tradmarks of First Star Software, Inc. © 1984, 1988 Kemco/First Star Software, Inc.

Star Voyager is a trademark of Acclaim Entertainment, Inc. © 1986, 1987 ASCII Corp. Game pak © 1987 Acclaim Entertainment, Inc.

Strider is a trademark of Capcom USA, Inc. © 1989 Capcom USA, Inc.

Super Mario Bros. and Mario Bros. are registered trademarks of Nintendo of America, Inc. © 1988 Nintendo of America, Inc.

Super Mario Bros. 2 is a trademark of Nintendo of America, Inc. © 1988 Nintendo of America, Inc.